*f***P**

Dream BIG!

*A Roadmap for Facing Life's Challenges
and Creating the Life You Deserve*

Deborah Rosado Shaw

The Free Press

New York London Toronto Sydney Singapore

*f*P
The Free Press
A Division of Simon & Schuster
1230 Avenue of the Americas
New York, NY 10020

Designed by Brooke Zimmer Koven
Manufactured in the United States of America

10   9   8   7   6   5   4   3   2   1

Library of Congress Cataloging-in-Publication Data

Shaw, Deborah Rosado
Dream big! : a roadmap for facing life's challenges and creating the
life you deserve /
Deborah Rosado Shaw. p. cm.
1. Women--psychology. 2. Women--Conduct of life. 3. Success.
4. Self -actualization (Psychology) I.Title.

HQ1206.S468 2001
158.1'082--dc21   00-052078

ISBN 0-684-86799-0

This book is dedicated to my sons:
Jason, Andrew, and Matthew —
three incredible human beings who have enriched my journey
with so much love,
support, and joy.
And to my brother,
for teaching me about courage and the gift of life.

Contents

Contents

Contents

Contents

INTRODUCTION

By opening this book, you are admitting that you have a dream. You're acknowledging the restless spirit deep inside who prods you to do more than sit back in a spectator's seat.

Maybe you've been a star player and know it's time to change your game, but you aren't sure how to go about it.

Maybe you've been the great pretender, trying to convince yourself that your current life is all you ought to have.

Maybe you've been trying to eat or work your desire away, but nothing satisfies the hunger for a life that's filled with joy and vitality.

Perhaps you've lost touch with the secret to effervescent living: integrity . . . integrity that begins within, being honest with yourself about who you are and what you need and want.

Do you have a thousand voices clamoring in your ear— the voices of family, friends, and society—voices of those with their own ideas about what constitutes "the good life" and who are eager to define an ideal world for you? Are these messages so loud that you can no longer hear the soft, inner voice that whispers to you alone?

Are you stopped, stuck, hesitating? Do you ache to begin your journey or change destinations, but are filled with fear? And even if you could summon the courage, do you not know where to begin?

I've been there, groping my way like a blind woman in

the dark. The truth is that there is no "jiffy lube" for life. Living out a dream includes months of not knowing, times when the uncertainty rattles so loudly you can't hear your inner voice. There are no answers out there. The answers are all inside. You bring them about for yourself.

You already have the courage, wells of reserves you've never tapped. And within these pages I'll share some of my personal discoveries and give you navigational help to chart your own course.

But with knowledge comes responsibility. With these newfound gems will come the need for a decision. You must ask yourself: What is more painful—moving forward and taking the necessary risks, or staying where I am, masking the truth?

Consider this: You have a burning desire because it's your *right* to have it.

Consider that your restlessness might be only the symptom and living your dream the cure.

Whether you want to take your company public, sell cookies out of your kitchen, land that new job, or start a movement to change the world, this book is for you.

Today I live a life I couldn't have imagined back when I was growing up in the Bronx, poor and powerless, a chubby girl with glasses and a wild streak. A girl who snipped fancy labels out of rummage bin dresses and sewed them into her secondhand clothes. A child who, despite being told "No" by everyone around her, dreamed of a bigger world full of "Yes" possibilities.

I might be a self-made woman and the CEO of my own company. I might have designed and closed deals with some of the biggest companies in the world. At thirty-eight, I might be a millionaire who can choose to not work another day in my life.

But I'm also a combination of all the girls of my past, stacked inside me like Russian dolls: the four-year-old lost in Harlem struggling to find her way out, the terrified adolescent at Bronx's Taft High who ran home every day to avoid being assaulted by gangs, the naive college freshman at Wellesley whose roommate didn't want to live with a ghetto kid.

The woman I am today is the result of those girls' experiences—their challenges, their hardships, and their victories.

Like most women, I've learned about success the hard way, on my own. There were times when I lay awake worrying about my kids, shook in my high heels in front of audiences, and felt so lonely that I sat in my robe on the edge of my bathtub and cried my face off. I've had to fall on that same face, push against my limits, and let go of the images I had in my head about successful women—images conjured by others.

And although I've defined and created my own success, I still haven't arrived at the place where everything is smooth and easy. There is no such destination, not as long as you're alive.

Sometimes when I'm on a plane, flying to speak at a conference, I look down at my fancy shoes and realize how far I've come. When I was growing up in the South Bronx, I used to stare at my scuffed hand-me-down loafers and dream of soft, pretty shoes that fit and didn't pinch my toes and rub blisters on my heels.

I grew up in a neighborhood that was among the poorest in the country, a place where you could get stabbed during a school bathroom break or die in your sleep from a stray bullet crashing through your wall. Back then I considered myself lucky to make it home from school in one piece. Pretty shoes were a luxury, to be bought only after food and heat were taken care of. But that didn't keep me from wanting them.

As a girl, I often rode the bus through midtown New York, and I used to stare out at the glittering department store windows. I gazed at all the prosperous people in their beautiful clothes, walking through neighborhoods that were clean and safe. I tried to imagine their lives, which seemed so perfect from that bus window. And I asked myself: How can I get what they have?

I wanted everything I passed on that moving bus—not just the coats and the shoes in the windows, but the abundant life: choices, power, dignity.

I quickly realized that nobody was gonna give all that to me. People in my world were doing their best to just survive. If I was going to have a different life than the one I was living, I was going to have to get it for myself.

Now I'm able to buy any kind of shoe I want, for myself and for anyone in my family. I don't quite have Imelda Marcos's shoe mania, but let's just say I'm on a first-name basis with my local department stores' shoe sales staff. And I still remember how it felt to look at my feet in those scuffed hand-me-downs. The memory not only grounds me where I am today but reminds me where I came from. I often think of the many people who are still peering out windows like I did, dreaming of more.

There is nothing like the difficulties of childhood—and I don't know about you, but I'm still having a difficult childhood—to send you straight to the center of yourself. When faced with humbling challenges, you quickly learn what you're made of. You discover your strengths and weaknesses, your talents and limitations, what motivates you and what stifles you, which pieces of your past serve you and which hinder, which dreams for your future are realistic and which are nothing but fantasies.

When you arrive at this place of self-awareness, you have the opportunity to practice self-acceptance—and, eventually, self-love. This unfolding and learning is a lifelong process, but for me it's the only true measure of success. "Making it" is journeying to that place, sacred and unique to us all, and loving the person we find there. It's loving and embracing all the little girls inside the Russian doll.

Each stage of my life has taught me skills and strategies that have helped me create the success I live today. These skills are learnable. I want to share them so you can utilize them for yourself.

You won't find any instant personality or lifestyle makeovers in this book. I don't believe in them. Ebenezer Scrooge might have changed overnight, but, sadly, such transformations often take much longer for the rest of us.

Think of me as a rich aunt who's left you a nice inheritance; you still have to do your own work, but you get a leg up on the journey.

As a woman who wants success, you're going to have to work differently for it than a man. Doing it "in a skirt" takes a distinct set of skills, skills we've designed and created on the go. And although the good ol' boys club is showing signs of stress, a gender-blind world has not yet arrived.

Yet, the greatest obstacles aren't the ones you encounter from the outside, they're the ones living under your skin. Our worst enemies aren't discrimination, unequal pay, and testosterone. They are fear, pride, fantasy, underdeveloped skills, and stifled creativity.

In the following pages, you'll learn strategies to:

- ◆ Claim your power
- ◆ Use fear
- ◆ Make a move . . . any move
- ◆ Get focused
- ◆ Build a safety net
- ◆ Take something or somebody on
- ◆ Strut your stuff
- ◆ Network strategically
- ◆ Take the plunge
- ◆ *Dream Big* and live it now

You can define and create your own success. But that special world, all your own, isn't waiting for you somewhere over a rainbow. No tornado is going to sweep you into it someday. You bring that world into being each day.

And every step enables you to open yourself up to great joy, unimagined happenings, and magical discoveries.

Chapter 1

Claim Your Power

*"One can never consent to creep when one feels
an impulse to soar."*

—HELEN KELLER

This is it.

Your life.

You'll never pass this way again.

And it's a journey that can be fueled by an infinite source of energy and strength, the same power that pushes a blade of grass through a crack in a concrete slab. This force is readily available, free-flowing, and abundant. And we all need to utilize this power if we are to enjoy the extraordinary life we were intended to have.

But you know what? No one can give you power. Only *you* can claim what's yours.

I HAD ARRIVED! BUT WHERE?

Anyone who saw me standing at the podium during the awards ceremony that day would have called me a success. I had beaten the odds! I was living an impossible future.

Without money or contacts, this girl from the South Bronx had built a successful enterprise and enduring relationships with some of the most powerful businesspeople in the world.

But as I stood at the podium of the Waldorf-Astoria, I felt three feet tall again, an imposter, a girl dressed up in a woman's fancy clothes.

No one sitting in the audience had any idea that I'd been forcing myself to get out of bed for months, that I had spent the previous year struggling with depression and self-doubt.

I had lost touch with little Debbie Rosado, the Puerto Rican girl who played the organ pedals with her shoes off, who wouldn't sit still in the church pews, who challenged her Sunday school teachers with endless questions like "If God's fair, how come we've got to do without?"

But in those days and weeks before my experience at the Waldorf, I had begun dreaming of that girl again. As though waking from a drugged sleep, I had started to see my surroundings—the opulent parties, luxurious homes, and elegant people—through her eyes, eyes that were piercing and completely honest, as only a child's vision can be.

I could hear her asking me: *Is this what it's all about? Is this what we struggled for?*

Her questions went unanswered. Something was askew. I was no longer listening to that precious, all-important part of myself. Foolishly, I had begun to think that I had "succeeded" in leaving her behind.

I'd not only moved away from my old neighborhood, I'd also moved away from myself. I'd become lost in the Never-Never Land of Getting and Spending.

I'd been so focused on escaping poverty that I'd lost sight of the defiant, streetwise girl inside who knew what really mattered to her and to me, and who wasn't interested in anyone else's version of success.

She wanted more than a Jacuzzi and a drawer full of jewelry to show for her efforts, her years of sacrifice.

She was reminding me that I needed to align my values with my daily world. But I wasn't sure how to go about it.

In the midst of this, as I was flipping through a magazine, I spotted an announcement about the Women of Enterprise Award sponsored by Avon and the U.S. Small Business Administration. This award was given to female business owners who had overcome significant odds to build a successful enterprise.

Some instinct (and a bit of prodding from my eldest son, Jason) made me pick up my pen and apply.

The application I received in the mail asked some thought-provoking questions:

What is your personal definition of success?
At what point did you say to yourself, "I've made it"?
What matters most in your life?

As I contemplated these questions, I thought how ironic it would be if a woman mired in depression and self-doubt won such an award.

Yet I did.

A month later I opened the notice from Avon, read the first word—"Congratulations"—and whooped out loud. I was going to be honored in front of 1,400 luminaries at the Waldorf-Astoria. I'd been awarded a stay in New York, with theater, dinner, media appearances, a cash gift, and a makeover.

I had reached out to the light, and the universe had conspired to help me. Even through my depression, I managed to float up to the sunlit clouds.

But once I was seated in the Waldorf's grand ballroom the day of the awards luncheon, looking around at the crystal chandeliers and the impeccably dressed crowd, I found myself growing increasingly anxious. The world might have been honoring me, but no one had any idea what I had been going through inside.

Sitting with the audience in the dark, I watched my fragmented self flicker before me in a "this-is-your-life" video Avon had prepared. There I stood, working with Bill Blass in his luxurious office, surrounded by mannequins draped in opulent fabrics, his innovative sketches, chalks and pens—the tools of a true artist.

Another image flashed across the screen: my parents, heartbreakingly young, cradling me, their firstborn, as if I were the most precious thing in the world. Other pictures quickly followed: Deborah Rosado Shaw as a disgruntled teenager, proud business owner, frazzled mother—standing on a dirty street in Harlem, on Madison Avenue, and on the lush grounds of Wellesley College's lakeside campus.

Some people say you see your life like this, scene by scene, in one endless shining moment, right before you die. I was humbled by the honor of being able to view my journey before passing on. And that experience altered the rest of my life.

When it was my turn to speak, my ears roared and my legs shook as I made my way up to the podium. When I looked out over the glittering crowd, the old voices I had battled all my life came thundering back at me: *You don't belong here. Who do you think you are?*

In the audience were assembled all the components of my life, a stew of people I had never dared mix together before.

There was my father, a Methodist minister, and my mother, a caseworker with demons of her own. There were my three sons, each born in a different stage of my evolution; my husband, Steve; my younger brother; and my best friend, Doreen.

There was Flora Davidson, a college professor who had taught me one of life's toughest lessons by pushing me to go farther than I had thought possible.

There were my business associates, whom I had always kept in the cubicle of my business life, and the editor of an important trade publication.

Nearly every person who was responsible in any way for my success, some who knew me intimately and others who barely knew me at all, were together in one room for the first time.

Then I was introduced and, bolstered by the applause, stepped into the spotlight and began speaking: "Today I share with you a very sweet moment. A moment that speaks to the power of the human spirit and what can be accomplished when we dare to dream. . . . "

As I began telling my story, the pieces of my life that had been neatly compartmentalized before began to meld. With every word I recovered another piece of myself. Although I was speaking to the audience, I was speaking even more to myself, relating what I saw so clearly. By integrating the components of my life, by recognizing and embracing all the people I had been and the experiences I had lived, good and bad, I gained access to my own source of power.

That power had always been there, just waiting to be claimed.

CHOOSE OR LOSE

When you were growing up, some fool probably told you that you could grow up to be anything you wanted. And, like most kids, you intended to be a doctor, a rock star, an Oscar-winning actress . . . *and* president of the United States. Well, now you're a grown-up, and you have to throw out the assumption that you can do anything and be anybody by simply believing it.

This form of positive thinking is a lot of bull. It's a myth and a destructive one, usually promoted by individuals who are selling instructional audiotapes, videos, motivation seminars, and yes . . . even books. Although there are many wonderful self-help products on the market, beware of those that tell you that you can have and do it all. It just isn't so. This cruel lie encourages us to waste our energy trying to do things we can never succeed at instead of helping us to make choices about where to put our efforts.

In case you missed the news, *Superwoman is dead!* She had a nervous breakdown and got committed to the crazy house, where she expired. We live in a world of infinite possibilities, but we have only so many days and hours. We can conjure thousands of desires and wishes, but we have the energy and resources to pursue only the few that are crucial to us.

There's a unique, personal form of success that can be yours alone, one that will generate happiness and fulfillment. But you have to make choices, sometimes tough ones, on your way to defining and creating that success.

I know what it's like, trying to do and be everything.

When I was living in California, I had three babies under four years of age and I spent most of my day doing . . . too much. When I traveled to the East Coast on business, I regularly took my sons along. I wanted to make sure they continued to have contact with both sets of grandparents. I would drop them off at one set of relatives, rush around New York having meetings and eating lunch, hurry back for dinner, and then take them to the next set. I was in a placating mode, a do-it-all-at-once mode, and I was a wreck.

On one trip, as I was struggling out the door with car seats and luggage, a pair of my underpants fell out of a duffel bag. I picked them up and stuck them into the waistband of my slacks until I got into the car. But once I was inside the car something else grabbed my attention and I forgot about them. I walked around—knickers exposed—in the airport, during the plane ride, and all the way through the terminal on the other side. It wasn't until we finally reached our destination that I had a moment to catch a breath and relax. I glanced down, and there they were . . . my latest Victoria's Secret acquisition, hanging out the side of my slacks. Of course, the kids hadn't told me; they were too little to care about such trivialities as modesty, and they were used to their mother's rushing around like a lunatic. Still, I had to laugh. And then I had to take a hard look at what I was doing to myself.

Sometimes you just have to stop and take a deep breath and say, "What am I trying to do? Be all things to all people?"

Well, you know what? You can't.

This clunker you're living in has only so much mileage. By trying to accomplish too much, you spread your resources thin and wind up running on empty . . . with too little attention paid to the most important things. Family and those closest to your heart suffer. You suffer. And eventually your health—mental, emotional, and physical—will suffer.

Realizing these things, the next time I visited I rearranged my schedule. I got a hotel room and asked the grandparents to visit us. I got a friend to baby-sit the kids. I streamlined my schedule so I had no more than two meetings a day.

I turned down the heat so the pot wouldn't boil over. No, I didn't get a prize that year for the most devoted daughter-in-law. There was no award for my homemade banana bread or pumpkin pie. My hairdo didn't receive rave comments—my hair looked like a disheveled mop most of the time. But I took pleasure from my kids and concentrated on my business. Those were my priorities, and I stuck to them. I had learned to invest my resources wisely. I had realized the importance of spending "me" on the things closest to my heart.

WHAT'S YOUR VERSION
OF THE GOOD LIFE?

Before you can decide where to "invest" your precious assets—your time, your energy, your money, even your affections—get to know what matters most to *you*. Because this is different for everyone, you must ask your quiet, inner self: What do I really care about?

It might take you a while to answer that question; it did me.

Even at the height of my so-called high life in California, I would stand at the supermarket checkout and leaf through the magazines with a heavy heart.

I already had a lot of good things in my life. According to society, I had "arrived," and I should have been happy. But I still wasn't satisfied.

I used to love reading home magazines, but I eventually stopped subscribing to them because they made me feel so inadequate. I have a nice house, but it doesn't belong in *Architectural Digest* or *Metropolitan Home*. I live in a house where kids knock holes into the walls with their hockey sticks.

And forget the beauty magazines—I'd spent half my youth following diagrams for shading my eyelids and highlighting my cheekbones, but I never looked like the girls on the covers of *Seventeen* or *Vogue*.

The next time you're reading one of those magazines, glance up and look at the people around you. You quickly realize what ridiculous fantasies the world encourages. I remember a cartoon I saw once. In it, two old women are standing over the casket of a friend. "Poor Rosie," one says to the other. "She was only twenty pounds from her goal."

Think of all the fruitful ways you could spend the energy you now waste pursuing someone else's fantasy of perfection. You'll probably never be a size 4 or have flawless skin or drive a Jaguar, so why not focus on something concrete, something that's possible and has meaning for you?

FACE YOUR TRUTH

What really matters to me?

I could have saved myself plenty of tissues and Prozac if I'd paid more attention to this question.

I used to pull out of the driveway each morning with a sinking heart, looking at all the mothers standing at their front doors in bathrobes and jogging outfits. There they were, holding down the fort all day while I was kissing my kids and heading off to the corporate world.

Mind you, I was always there for the big events in my children's lives. I made it my business to show up for anything important. But I still kicked myself around about other things. Was it really all right to travel so much? What about not being home for a week in a row?

My kids seemed healthy and fine to me and to everyone else, but I began constructing dramatic scenarios in my mind. In these scenarios my children were secretly unhappy, pining for a mother who waited for them in an apron at the door.

Delay and dramatize, this song-and-dance routine was my main act. I delayed action and dramatized everything: *I can't take on this project. What are the boys gonna think if I tell them I have to go away again? Can I miss two football games in a row? And what about Andrew's concert?*

And on and on with no end in sight. My theatrics grew until I decided I couldn't live through one more curtain call.

I marched into the living room, where my three sons were sitting over their homework, and announced that we were going to have a heart-to-heart.

I put my cards on the table. "There's some stuff I want to get done in the world," I told them. "I love you guys with all my heart, and I also love being in business—the ups and downs, the challenges, the excitement. Sometimes I wish I could be someone else, but I'm sorry, this is it. I need you guys to accept me for who I am."

Blah, blah, blah, I went on.

When I finally ran out of steam I looked at them. They sat there looking slightly amused.

"What?" I said.

"Why are you telling us this?" Jason, my oldest son, said "We know already."

"Yeah," the middle one, Andrew, agreed. "You're our mom. You've always been this way. We're fine."

I stood a moment, almost panting. "But there are things you don't have that other kids do," I tried, hoping to kick myself a little more.

"So what? There are lots of things we have that they don't," said Matthew, the youngest.

I had to laugh. They had come to terms with who I was long before. I was the one who had been twisting around to whip myself.

That speech was not a waste of time, however. Far from it. Fessing up gave me a freedom I never had before. I was able to stop concocting imaginary obstacles and fictions.

The good news about living your dream is that you contribute not only to yourself but to everyone around you. And you learn to seek your own counsel instead of casting about for approval from everyone else.

You're the one who has to be clear about what a good life looks like. And you have to be able to hold on to your dream through the dark and painful moments.

That's a lesson Nancy Archuleta discovered for herself.

When Nancy was in high school, a vocational counselor told her that she'd never amount to anything. "You're just a poor Mexican," the counselor said when Nancy expressed her wish to go to college.

But Nancy didn't believe that.

She had another image of herself—as an educated, successful woman—and she held on to it through years of discouragement and poverty.

Even when her life was at its lowest, when she was a high school dropout, a battered wife, a mother of three before she was nineteen, Nancy held on to her dream. She told herself that she wasn't just her circumstances and that one day she would find a way to prove it.

Nancy Archuleta kept the flame of her ambition burning inside even when fate and circumstance conspired to blow it out.

After years of struggle, Nancy managed to escape her marriage. She juggled several jobs to support her kids and finish her education. Then she invested every dollar she could scrape together into a systems management company, Mevatec. Eventually she was named president.

When she realized that this was just a token position and

that she'd been awarded it so the company could gain minor-ity-woman-owned status, she didn't throw up her hands and surrender. She remained focused and managed to wrestle control of the company from her partner and become its true leader.

Today she is chairman and CEO of Mevatec Corporation, a $62 million integration/software development firm and one of the country's fastest growing Hispanic-owned companies.

Nancy didn't just endure. She didn't just prevail. She triumphed.

This is what you can accomplish when you face your truth.

HIDDEN POWER ZAPPERS

Comparing

It's human nature to peek over the fence and note the lush, green grass on the other side. But comparisons aren't only unsatisfying, they're empty.

Compared to others in California, my life looked the spitting image of happy and affluent. But how it stacked up with others meant nothing . . . because it was unfulfilling to me.

You can't know what someone else's life is really like. Stop comparing! Use the time to cultivate your own garden instead.

Justifying

As women we're often experts on the fruitless art of justification. *Just let me explain! Hear me out a minute!* But the only one who needs justifying to is . . . you! I wasted a lot of time and energy trying to explain why my business was important to me, even to people who weren't central to my life. Then I started being straight with myself and stopped feeling the need. So will you.

Judging

The brother of justifying is judging. They're the dynamic duo of time wasting and energy zapping. When they crop up, get out the weed whacker and cut 'em down.

If you're busy rating others, you're probably denigrating yourself. Knock it off, and get focused on living your dream instead.

Accept others' right to choose and don't engage in their judgment of your choices.

STAKING OUT YOUR CLAIM

Be Still

Self-reflection allows us to gain insights into our dreams and desires. By being quiet, asking ourselves meaningful questions, and remaining open to the answers, we enhance our self-knowledge. Relaxing the mind and finding a place of inner peace helps us tune in to our deepest longings.

Ask Tough Questions

Take a deep breath and relax. Close your eyes and ask yourself:

What are my nonnegotiable values?
Am I acting in ways that reflect my beliefs?
What are the barriers?
Which barriers have I created?
What are my strengths and weaknesses?
What works in my life? What doesn't?
What's missing?

TURNING ON THE JUICE

Access to your own power and freedom is available through the experiences that bring you joy and meaning. What brings meaning to your day? What really turns you on?

- Spiritual devotion
- Creative expression
- Career success
- Health
- Material prosperity
- Family harmony
- Helping others
- Physical fitness
- Leisure activities
- Friendship
- Romantic love

With these in mind, imagine your own version of a perfect future:

◆ What are you doing?
◆ Where are you?
◆ Who is there with you?

Fast-back in time to the present, right now. What must you do to claim your power, the power you possess to create your life? Many obstacles slow us down or stop us altogether. But the important question is: What's stalling *you*?

Chapter 2

Stop Fighting Fear

"You must do the thing you think you cannot do."
— ELEANOR ROOSEVELT

In the horror movies I watched as a girl, the woman always runs away from whatever she's afraid of—whether it's a monster, a killer, or a storm. And when she runs, she does it ineptly—in high heels or in a halfhearted, hysterical way. Invariably, she stumbles and falls. And that's where she ends up, in a heap with a twisted ankle, passively waiting to be finished off.

With images like these in our heads, no wonder so many of us keep fighting fear.

As women we have been taught to stick to the straight and narrow, to head for the smoothly paved, well-lit, safe, and secure highway. But it's the rough road that tests your skills and leads you past sights that the interstate bypasses.

It's by taking chances, by wandering out into the darkness, that you discover what you're made of.

LIVING ON THE MEAN STREETS— *REALLY MEAN*

I was afraid all the time when I was a girl.

Nights in our neighborhood were full of police sirens, fights, and gunshots. Gang members roamed our streets and ruled our corners. Junkies nodded off on the stoop in front of our house.

When I was nine, the body of a dead man appeared in front of the church where my father was a preacher. In the inner city, bodies, like garbage, aren't regularly picked up. Day after day, he lay there, stinking and bloating. I kept thinking, *This man must be someone's father or son or brother.* But no one claimed him. The message was clear: He didn't matter, and neither did the rest of us.

Eventually, my mother called a local television station and caused such a ruckus that the man was finally taken away. But before he was removed, I had to pass his body each day on my way to school. And as I did so, I made myself a promise: *When I grow up, I won't live like this—and neither will my kids.*

WHEN HOME IS NOT A HAVEN

I didn't even feel safe at home. Throughout my childhood, my mother suffered from asthma, epilepsy, and what I now realize was depression. Whenever there was stress, she had an attack, and there was *always* some kind of stress in our lives. If it wasn't the furnace breaking down, it was the hot water running out or some vagrant banging on our back door.

While other families went out to dinner on Friday nights, my mother had seizures. She grew disoriented or lost consciousness. We couldn't keep ceramics and glassware around because she was always breaking things.

But she was able to rally for other people's emergencies. She could lead rent strikes and walk junkies up and down the street to keep them conscious until the police arrived.

And then we had an emergency of our own. When he was four, my younger brother, Josh, was diagnosed with a life-threatening, degenerative kidney disorder. The prognosis: He would lose kidney function and have to go on dialysis. The doctors told us he might die.

I found this news almost impossible to accept. My innocent, adorable brother, who my sister and I babied when my mother wasn't well. Sick?

At night, I stared at him as he slept, terrified he might stop breathing if I closed my eyes. How had this happened? Why him and not me? How could someone so young and alive have anything wrong with him?

From observing my brother, I learned about courage. I watched him get up in the morning and face his uncertain future. I saw him grow up in the middle of hospital stays and doctors' visits. I watched him struggle with the isolated life of a sick child.

I knew he was terrified every time he went in for a checkup, but he went anyway, in spite of it.

From his courageous example, I saw that the best way to face fear was to march right up to it, not to shrink away or try to hide.

Throughout my life, whenever I've become discouraged or frightened I've thought of Josh. And the enormity of what he faced and the bravery he showed would humble me all over again.

LEARNING COURAGE FROM EVERYDAY HEROES

I saw another kind of courage in my mother, whose love for Josh focused and invigorated her.

As a girl, my mother had dreamed of becoming a doctor. But her family said, "You're a girl. Why go to college? You're just going to get married and have kids," and they sent her brother instead.

But she managed to salvage part of her dream by studying chemistry. Now, all those years later, she found a way to utilize what she'd learned. She researched my brother's disease and fought with the doctors, insisting they try the newest approach, which would allow his illness to run its course without the use of drugs. My mother bet on this new thinking, and her gamble paid off. Because of her courageous battle on his behalf, my brother was able to mature and live a more normal life.

Seeing my brother so weak and sick made death real for me. It wasn't a word or idea anymore. I wanted to protect Josh, to shield and heal him. But I couldn't. The most I could do was fight my own fears as he fought his, to seize the life I had and cherish it in his honor.

INNOCENCE VIOLATED

Living with uncertainty became a way of life in my family. The only peace I could find was in the church sanctuary, where I slipped away to play the organ, an antique with gold-etched pipes that had been transported in pieces from Germany. I loved the big sounds I created pumping the pedals in the half dark. I felt lifted out of our crumbling neighborhood into another, lofty world.

But even that peace didn't last.

When I was nine, my father hired a relative to work as a sexton in the church. He was a friendly man, about my father's age, with a wife and family of his own. I barely noticed him until one afternoon, when I realized that he'd begun hanging around whenever I practiced. Each day, he moved a little closer.

"What're you playing?" he asked me one afternoon.

"A hymn."

"Which one?"

I felt him press into me as he looked over my shoulder at the music. His touch sent off an alarm, but I tried to ignore it. He was an adult, a member of my family. He'd never do anything wrong.

He began leaving his mop in the corner and sitting beside me on the bench.

"You play so pretty," he murmured close to my ear. His breathing sounded ragged, like he'd just run up a flight of stairs.

As the weeks passed by, he began bringing me bags of chocolates and peppermints.

"Sweets for the sweet girl," he said, and draped his arm around me. He sat so close that I could smell the oil in his hair. He stared at the sheet music, but I could tell he was really focused on something else.

I believed in God. I told myself that nothing bad would ever happen in his house. And just in case I was wrong, I prayed that this man would go away. But he didn't go away; he just grew bolder. Even when I tried to evade him, he always seemed to find me.

One afternoon while I was practicing late, I felt him enter the room behind me. I told myself that if I just kept moving my hands everything would be all right.

I kept playing as I felt him approach. I kept playing as his shadow fell across the keys. When he put his hands on my shoulders, I stopped playing. My face felt as if it were covered with ice.

Something terrible happened that day. He pressed himself on me, and his hands violated my innocence. I waited for God's lightning to strike him down, but heaven was silent.

I reported the incident to my father, hoping he'd rage against this man and kill him. But he turned the other cheek and claimed that God would deal with the offender in the afterlife.

The man was fired. That was all; he was no longer in our lives.

After that, I looked at the world differently. I felt that no one was going to miraculously appear to help me when I was in trouble, not even God. I realized that the world was a scary place, and I was going to have to confront it—and my fears—myself.

USE FEAR

When you experience fear, your body actually releases glucose, adrenaline, and other energy-producing chemicals. Your heart rate increases, your breathing becomes shallow, you are hyper-alert. This energy can be redirected and used to face your challenges.

That is exactly what Marion Luna Brem learned to do. At thirty-two, she found herself newly divorced, with no résumé, no marketable skills, and two children to support.

And she was battling a life-threatening cancer without health insurance.

There were a number of ways Marion could have handled these setbacks. She could have crawled into bed and taken the phone off the hook. She could have slid into despair. She could have handed her kids off to her mother and asked her to care for them.

Instead she confronted her fear and decided to act in spite of it.

So Marion decided to try her hand at sales. Between chemotherapy treatments, she began applying to automobile dealerships. When she walked into showrooms, a pale woman in a pantsuit, and said she wanted a job selling, salesmen looked at her as if she'd landed from Mars. She was laughed at when she wasn't dismissed out of hand.

"Broads can't sell cars," one salesman told her.

But Marion persisted. Even as she suffered the side effects of chemotherapy, she put on her makeup and headed out the door. She walked right past her fear of being destitute, of dying from cancer, of leaving her children without a mom, and she continued knocking on doors.

Finally, a manager at one of the dealerships agreed to give her the chance she needed.

Now, ten years later, Marion is the founder of several companies, including Love Chrysler, one of the largest auto dealerships in the South.

But she says that the most successful day of her life was the first day she walked into her new job, wearing a wig and carrying inside herself the pride of what she had faced and conquered.

HAVE A GOOD SHAKE IN YOUR BOOTS

When you summon the courage to travel to the center of your fear, you often find that there's nothing there. But you have to *act* before you can discover that.

When you're hanging from a jungle gym you have to let go of the rung for a moment to move forward. No doubt about it; it's scary. There's an instant when you could fall. But you have to hang with fear to reach the other side.

So many of us are just hanging on the same rung, trying to decide whether we have the nerve to reach for the next one. Some of us simply want to stay off the jungle gym completely and hide in our little caves. But hiding out won't get you anywhere.

If you're not doing things that make you shake in your boots, you're missing some of the fun and—even more of the opportunities—of living.

For many, many years, one of my biggest personal fears was public speaking. Yet one autumn day in 1996 I found myself driving a rental car through the back roads of Arkansas on my way to speak at a Saturday morning business meeting at Wal-Mart. If you've never heard of these famous meetings, they're part motivation and part accountability sessions. In an arena-style theater, 1,200 of Wal-Mart's most senior managers recount the business of the week and evaluate their performance around the world.

It's a place where all kinds of people are invited to share new ideas. Garth Brooks, President Bush, and Colin Powell have all been invited. And—unbelievably—me.

I still found it hard to accept that I was going to be speaking to some of the most powerful merchants in the world about who I was and where I was from. Standing on that podium-free platform, flanked left, right, and rear by Wal-Mart's CEO and executive team, this city girl provided evidence to support their business tenet that "ordinary people can achieve extraordinary things."

Three hours before my presentation, I was so apprehensive about the speech that I half hoped a tornado would appear on the horizon and blow my rented car into a ditch. It was the same terror I'd felt when I used to walk to school through my violent neighborhood. Huddled in my coat, I had tried to make myself as small as possible, hoping that the junior high school boys who mugged us kids for lunch money and bus passes wouldn't notice me. But every day I heard the boys bear down on me, the slap of their shoes on the pavement as they approached from behind. Waiting for them, I always felt a sense of dread. Then I was knocked down, and my bus pass and lunch money were torn away. No sandwich for lunch that day and a long walk home. This happened so often that I stopped telling anyone about it.

But I was a child then. I *had* to go to school and face those kids. Even then, I realized that education was my only way out.

Driving through Arkansas, I was seized with the same fear, but I realized that I was in an entirely different situation. One, I had the power of choice. And more important, that little girl was really safe now. I was a grown woman and a mother; I would never let anyone hurt her that way again.

And this situation was very different. Even if I fell on my face in front of this crowd, my life waited for me unaffected back home in New Jersey. My children would be safe, my business intact, and I wouldn't become a bag lady.

So even though I was shaking in my shoes, I had chosen this. I was voluntarily taking a plunge into the fear to see what I might discover.

And you know what? I not only lived through it; it was wonderful! I focused on the audience's needs; how they might be inspired to champion an associate's capacity for greatness. And my message was received with more enthusiasm than I could have hoped for. I used the energy released by my fear to fuel my presentation and give it passion.

Grappling with fear yields strength and confidence. Every time you survive a frightening experience, you renounce fear's grip.

These moments of letting go can yield breakthrough results.

PRIDE KILLS OPPORTUNITY

Sometimes we're so busy trying to look good that we end up relinquishing some of life's sweetest moments.

Once, when I was at the posh Frederic Fekkai salon in New York City getting primped for an interview on CNN, I looked over and saw the trademark red hair of a business icon sitting right next to me. It was Charlotte Beers, the legend who ran the advertising giant Ogilvy & Mather.

There were few businesspeople in the world I was more eager to meet. But I let the moment pass. For more than two hours, I failed to muster up the guts to introduce myself.

Why?

There are so many things that stopped me.

Maybe I didn't want to introduce myself to this Madison Avenue superstar with lavender goo running down the side of my face. Maybe I was afraid that if I, a total stranger, stuck out my hand, she'd think I was crazy. Maybe it was just an instant replay of the old voices that have always whispered nasty lies to me: *Who do you think you are? Why do you think anyone wants to meet you?*

Whatever the reason, I didn't follow my impulse and take the move that was right there, waiting to be taken. It was a missed opportunity, pure and simple, with someone who completely intrigued me. God knows where it might have led. I could have established a successful business relationship with her, or we could have simply shared a moment of personal connection, woman to woman. I'll never know what might have happened.

Fear is an unpleasant sensation, and sometimes we hesitate, waiting for the feeling to subside before we act. But we can't avoid fear. Yes, it's uncomfortable, but it's also a healthy, even necessary, part of living an extraordinary life.

The challenge is to act in spite of it.

BULLETPROOF WAYS
TO SURRENDER AND WIN

Harness Your Fear

When we were children, our parents used fear as a tool to keep us from doing something. "You'll break your neck if you climb that tree!" they said. Our challenge as adults is to use fear as the fuel to get things done. Raw, unused fear can eat away at us, causing countless miseries, even life-threatening illnesses. But when we learn to harness and direct our fear, it provides the power we need to live our dreams.

- Kara J., a businesswoman who suffered anxiety attacks whenever she made a presentation, became an advocate for young handicapped women who couldn't speak for themselves.
- Dana R., who spent a lifetime fighting abandonment issues after growing up in an orphanage, found peace by bringing foster children into her home.
- Laura L., attacked as a young woman, turned to tae kwon do and now teaches self-defense to girls.

Focus Outside Yourself

Focusing outside yourself is a great way to stop fighting fear and save your strength. We've all been inspired by people like Kara and Dana and Laura, women who have learned to master the art of halting fear in its tracks. And we've experienced moments of heroism in our own lives, when we were able to accomplish something we once thought was impossible. Just think of the Million Mom March.

My own fear of public speaking used to immobilize me. But I looked beyond myself and concentrated on how my experiences might inspire or empower another person. When I was invited to speak to an audience of fifty, I forced my lips to say "Yes" even though my fear was screaming "No!"

And I made myself do the same when I was asked to address a group of one hundred. When I realized it didn't kill me, I did it again and again. Now I have a wall papered with copies of the checks I've received from traveling around the country giving speeches.

How did I go from a stammering wreck with sweaty palms and heart palpitations to someone who feels at home behind a podium and even relishes TV interviews? I surrendered!

Build Your Resistance

One particularly effective weapon for neutralizing fear is to desensitize yourself to the situation that triggers the stress.

Choose a live situation—something that's really pressing you right now—perhaps pitching the bank for an increased line of credit. Then engage it, first in your head, then through various real-life settings. Begin with the least intimidating and work your way up to the most threatening.

Before you begin, be sure you've done your homework. Nothing defuses fear like knowing your stuff.

Step 1: Find a guinea pig.
- Be the first volunteer; deliver the pitch in front of a mirror.
- Then graduate to your dog, a fellow business owner, your accountant . . .

Step 2: Do a live test. Never open up on Broadway. Give your pitch to a lender you never intend to use. Get the real-life jitters, questions, and feedback.

Step 3: Create familiarity. To disarm fear, kill surprise.

- Visit the locale beforehand and meet your target— do it incognito, if necessary.
- If you can't get to the location beforehand, visit it in your mind. Feel the texture of the fabric on the chairs, smell your target's perfume, taste the coffee being served.

Step 4: Expect flawless execution. Feel the fear, the excitement. See yourself, dressed in your best suit— poised, strong, driven—bringing down the house.

Over time, you'll have greater access to the fortitude that permits you to stare fear in the face—no matter how imposing, threatening, or ugly it looks.

Remember . . . "No guts, no glory!"

Chapter 3

Make a Move

"The rewards go to the risk-takers, those who are willing to put their egos on the line and reach out—to other people and to a richer, fuller life for themselves."

—SUSAN ROANE

———————————————— ▬▬▬ ————————————————

I think you already know what will happen in your life if you don't make a move. Stuff. And very little of it to your design.

In case you haven't noticed, life has a way of continuing to happen with or without your consent. It pauses for nothing and no one. It is relentless.

While you're waiting, figuring out exactly what the next, right, winning move is, you might want to consider this: Waiting around will get you nowhere. Boldness wins the day.

I learned one of my most important life lessons about taking action when I was only four.

About 1965, in the heat of the civil rights struggle, my father was a student pastor in an African American United

Methodist church in Harlem. His plan was to train there and launch a new ministry with Spanish-language services for the growing Puerto Rican community. Trailing behind him, our family stuck out like the proverbial badly smashed thumb. Not that I was aware of this; as a four-year-old I began school without a clue that I wasn't black. But kids can be quick to teach you and cruel about their lessons.

My first day of kindergarten I was mistaken for a white girl, beaten soundly, and tossed out the door. Once the school door shut, it automatically locked me out, and I was alone in the schoolyard. No one answered my cries or knocks. I was completely on my own . . . lost . . . with no idea how to get home.

Standing there in the crisp, cool, September sunshine, I had my first lesson in survival. I realized that there was nothing for me to do but put one foot in front of the other. I picked up my book bag, chose a direction, and began walking.

I walked for what seemed like hours until I found myself on a commercial corner that looked familiar. There was a cigar store on my right and a diner on my left. And just beyond the diner I finally saw something I recognized—a Maxwell House coffee sign. I ran toward that sign with my heart in my throat, and just beyond it, there was the stoop of our apartment.

That day I taught myself one of the most critical lessons in life—and business: It is essential to move forward, even when no map exists. If I had waited for someone to take me by the hand and show me the way home—or to success—I might still be standing there with my book bag on my shoulder and a heart full of fear.

You have to get going, even if you aren't quite sure how to get where you want to be. As the old proverb says: "God can't steer a bicycle that isn't moving." Get your feet on the pedals and start those wheels turning. Feel the breeze on your cheeks, the sun on your back, the sweet fresh air filling your chest . . . and enjoy the journey.

PLAY YOUR HUNCHES

One of the first signposts you see on your journey, directing your path, might be a hunch. It's terribly important to play those hunches, even if they're a little scary, because hunches are really insights in disguise.

That's what Aubyn Burnside did.

At ten, Aubyn became the founder of Suitcases for Kids. She started the project after listening to her sister Leslie, a social worker, describe how foster children often move from home to home with all their belongings stuffed into garbage bags.

Aubyn thought about the message this sent to the children: If your whole life is shoved into a garbage bag, maybe you're nothing but garbage yourself. She was so bothered by this that she began to investigate ways to help foster kids gain self-esteem. Her idea: Wouldn't it be great if these kids could have their own suitcases to store their personal possessions no matter where they lived?

Then she acted. She asked friends and neighbors if they would donate the suitcases they had lying about, gathering dust, in their basements, garages, and attics.

Aubyn didn't form a committee. She didn't take a vote. She didn't ask permission. She just *did* it.

After speaking to local church and school groups, she soon expanded to state and national organizations. Before she knew it, thousands of suitcases had been donated and the project had expanded to fifty states and sixteen countries!

Aubyn didn't listen to voices that said: *You're too young. You don't know what you're doing. This has never been done before.* Instead, she did the most natural thing in the world. She followed a hunch and acted, even though she had no idea how she'd get to where she was headed. Her hunch was really a personal insight into others' needs. She was moved by someone else's circumstances and decided to do something about it. In the beginning of her journey, she must have had moments of doubt and uncertainty, but look at what she accomplished by pressing beyond her fears.

Aubyn Burnside and others like her are living proof that it's in the realm of uncertainty where you find life's greatest rewards and surprises.

BE BOLD

Over the years, I've made it my business to reach out and extend myself whenever I sense an opportunity.

But opportunities don't have Alice in Wonderland–type tags on them saying TAKE ME. They don't hurl themselves across your path. You have to be on the prowl for them.

One of my favorite moves is writing letters to people I find inspiring. It's a direct and personal way of making contact with someone who might otherwise be beyond my reach.

You'd be surprised what a few words and a thirty-four-cent postage stamp can produce.

One Friday afternoon, I found myself at O'Hare Airport

in a real funk. I had been traveling a lot, my meetings hadn't gone well, and I'd just missed my flight connection. I felt like a wrung-out rag.

When I start feeling like this, I head to a bookstore. Books have revived and encouraged me more times than I can count, starting back when I was a girl and used to escape with Nancy Drew mysteries.

That afternoon I wandered the Chicago airport's bookstore aisles. I picked up Lou Pritchett's *Stop Paddling and Start Rocking the Boat.* Pritchett is a business legend who by his own definition was once a soap salesman for Procter & Gamble. After a famed canoe ride with Wal-Mart founder Sam Walton, he designed the integrative system that links Wal-Mart and P&G.

Whenever you go through a Wal-Mart checkout with a box of Procter & Gamble laundry detergent, the code on the side of the box is electronically relayed to the company. This direct link helps P&G plan how much soap needs to be made and where it should be sent. This allows the company to plan production, invest resources, and buy raw goods and materials in an efficient manner.

Lou Pritchett is the architect of this system. Now that he's retired, he's one of the most sought-after business speakers in the world.

Standing there in the terminal leafing through Pritchett's book, I found his admonishment—you can't get anywhere unless you rock the boat—to be just what I needed to hear at that moment. Yes, it's hard, and you can fall on your face, he wrote, but you still have to do it. In a matter of minutes, his words had prodded me out of my funk.

I bought the book and got on the plane, still reading. I

don't remember either taking off or landing. Pritchett's book affected me so deeply that I did a little research and wrote him a letter when I arrived home.

The letter began: "I have just completed reading your book, again. As you hoped, your experiences have become a source of 'education, motivation and enlightenment' for me. . . ."

After introducing myself, I asked if he could assist me in locating someone to mentor me as an entrepreneur. I even enclosed a response form and a self-addressed envelope with my home address to make it easy for him to respond, then I stuck the whole thing in the mail before I could change my mind.

And as I got swallowed up by my daily life, I tucked the letter into the back of my mind.

Not long afterward, I came home from work and found a message on my answering machine from a man with a soft Southern accent: "Deborah, this is Lou Pritchett. If I were in business today, I would hire you sight unseen. Give me a call." And he left his number.

I stood there with my coat half off, staring at the phone as if it had just sprouted wings.

After I took a few deep breaths, I phoned him back. That call was the first in a series of conversations that became gifts to me. Lou liked my spunk and acknowledged my achievements. He also helped direct some of my energy.

Later, when I was invited to speak at Wal-Mart, what better person to share this with than Lou Pritchett, who knew all the players? Soon after he would lend his help again, when I first became a vendor to Wal-Mart.

IS ANYONE OUT THERE LISTENING?

Even if you're involved in what appears to be a one-way correspondence, don't underestimate its value. At the time it might seem that the other person isn't listening. But you don't always know what's happening on the other end. People—especially movers and shakers—are busy, and they might not always have the time to respond. But that doesn't mean they aren't reading your letters and appreciating the contact.

Marian Wright Edelman, the founder of the Children's Defense Fund, is one of the most powerful children's rights activists in the country. A recipient of the Medal of Freedom, this nation's highest civilian honor, she is a personal inspiration. I have followed her accomplishments for years, since she spoke at my Barnard College commencement. I've always felt I was a beneficiary of her valiant work in fighting for the welfare of children.

I wrote her notes over the years in response to a book she'd authored or a speech she'd given. At the same time I kept her abreast of my projects. Even though I didn't usually receive responses to my notes, I still felt we were involved in a kind of communication.

It turned out I was right. After I sent her an announcement of a recently won award, she sent me a personal letter that ended: "With deep thanks for all you've done and continue to do for children."

That letter, which I now have hanging on my office wall, has gotten me out of a mental or emotional gutter more times than I can say.

When I've been feeling down, I look up at it and think: *Marian Wright Edelman believes in you! You'd better get up off your butt and do something!*

GO AHEAD, TAKE A SPILL

It took me thirty-six years to learn how to ride a bike.

When I was a kid, a bike wasn't on my priority list. Later, when I could afford to buy any bike I wanted, I still didn't learn. I imagined all kinds of neighborhood embarrassments. I saw myself falling on my butt in front of a crowd of fancy garden club ladies: *Who's that? Oh, it's that lady who was just in the paper . . . you know, the one with the umbrella.* And no, there weren't any garden club ladies standing around in my backyard, which only goes to show how stupid these negative thoughts really are.

Being tormented by a particularly vivid imagination, I pictured myself sideswiping cars, skidding on ice, careening down a hill straight into traffic. I could even visualize myself lying in my casket wearing a white satin nightgown, a twisted bicycle wheel around my neck and the handlebars sticking . . . well . . . never mind.

Enviously, I watched from my car window as other people pedaled by, carefree, with wind in their hair. The longer I put off learning, the larger the task loomed in my tortured fantasies. It seemed as if everyone else was flying, while I was earthbound, held by my stupid fears.

Matthew, my youngest son, was the one who finally motivated me. He had noticed my pathetic, yearning look. "You can do it too, Mom," he told me, his big eyes filled with loving concern. "I'll help you." I had to do something. It's one thing to be a wimp, but it's quite another to let your kid catch you wimping out.

So I embarked. Sometimes you have to make a move, any move, to get started. I bought a bike, but the seat was uncomfortable. So I ordered a special wide-load seat that, to my everlasting thanks, took several weeks to arrive. When the seat came, it was too big and I had to order another. A few more weeks zoomed by before the right one appeared.

Of course, now that I had the seat squared away, I realized I needed a better helmet and additional pads for my chin and wrists and elbows. I knew I was concocting obstacles to delay that first ride, and so did my son.

"C'mon, Mom. Aren't you ready to ride your bike yet?" he kept asking. What could I do?

With every joint cushioned by foam, and my head encased in plastic, a million morbid fantasies dancing in my mind, I waddled out into the yard with my son. After looking around to make sure there were no garden party ladies watching, I wrapped my legs over the bike. I risked looking like an idiot and started pumping those pedals.

It was worth facing my fears just to see the smile my son gave me as he pedaled past.

"See," he said. "I knew you could do it!" After all the times I had said those words to him, it was a joy to have them returned to me.

It's taken three years, but now I can ride completely around my circular drive. Like Dustin Hoffman's character in *Rainman,* I'm "a very good driver." I'm still afraid to go downhill or cruise where there's traffic, but those are my next goals.

Left to my own devices, I might never have gotten on that bike. I could have lived my whole life without ever experiencing that exhilarating sensation, without having seen that look on my son's face, without pedaling in tandem with someone else as if it were the most natural thing in the world.

Now I'm thinking about a Harley.

Excuses are limitless. We can always create reasons to not make a move. Ask yourself right now:

- What "bicycle" have I longed to ride, but haven't, because of fear?
- What excuses have I created to keep me from pumping those pedals?
- How can I "override" those excuses and begin my journey?

MAKE LUCK HAPPEN

I fund a scholarship for young women at Taft High in the South Bronx, the school where I spent ninth and tenth grade in abject fear.

When I first started going to Taft, I was a chubby twelve-year-old freshman scared for her life. Taft was a school where you might walk into a bathroom and find a stabbed or overdosed classmate. It was a place where police in riot gear stood guard in the halls.

I remember so clearly what it felt like to live in terror, cut off from mainstream American culture, and I want to help other young people keep their eyes on their own personal prize—their future. But when the scholarship award ceremony came around, I was completely depleted. I had been traveling for weeks, and I was exhausted.

The last thing I felt like doing was leaving my comfortable suburban world and traveling to my old Bronx school, where it was still so dangerous that you had to pass through metal detectors and be escorted at all times.

I asked a girlfriend to go with me to the ceremony, but at the last minute, she canceled. Rather than face a drive to the Bronx alone, I was ready to send the check for the scholarship to the school. I even had my hand on the phone to call the messenger service pick up number. But then I looked up at Marian Wright Edelman's letter, and I put down the receiver and got dressed instead.

When I pulled up at Taft, a mob had formed outside, and security was everywhere. *Probably a drug overdose or a drive-by shooting,* I thought.

"What's happening out there?" I asked the secretary when I reached the principal's office.

"They're renaming the street," she said.

"To what?"

"Levin Way. After Jonathan Levin."

Then I understood; Jonathan Levin had been a beloved teacher at Taft High School before a former student murdered him.

As fate would have it, one of the issues I addressed in my comments that afternoon was how significant the teachers in my life had been. I talked about how instructors like Jonathan Levin made daily, potent deposits of hope in the lives of countless disenfranchised inner-city kids while expecting nothing in return.

That day was miserably hot, and the auditorium wasn't air-conditioned. Babies were crying. Restless children milled about the aisles. Sitting in that broiling, overcrowded audience on splintered wooden chairs were Levin's mother and his father, the CEO of Time-Warner, Gerald Levin.

The combined forces of courage and grief on their faces is something I'll never forget. Unlike many people, who might have become mired in self-pity or bitterness, the Levins showed up at Taft High School to award scholarship funds in the name of a son who had cared very much for the kids there.

My opportunity to meet and talk with the Levins was a privilege that might have never come my way if I had pulled the covers over my head as I had been inclined to do that morning. My reward for crawling out of bed was a rich experience that I will always remember. And I would like to believe that the meeting benefited the Levin family as well, showing them a living example of the difference their son had made to inner-city kids.

This kind of serendipity has happened to me again and again when I make the effort to cast my bread upon the waters. And I'm sure you've had similar experiences in your life. When you want to move forward and lack the power:

- Recall a time when you moved forward and found a better place.
- Focus on that success. A gamble paid off once, and a new one can pay off again.
- Remind yourself that all isn't as it seems. The seeds you planted are germinating beneath the soil, whether you can see any green or not.
- Don't wait until you "feel good" to move. It's the movement that creates the good feelings.

Never underestimate the power of one small step forward. One move on your part can cause a chain of events that you could never have predicted. But there's no way to discover this unless you make that move.

RISK LOSING

Of course, I've had to fold plenty of bad hands. But if I hadn't jumped back into the game, I wouldn't have had any wins.

One bold hand I dared to play was an introductory letter to the CEO of Sears. I described why I thought our companies were a perfect match and the mutually advantageous ways we could work together. I got a chilly reply from an underling, saying essentially, "Who do you think you are writing to our CEO? Don't call us, and we're certainly not going to call you."

I had a similar result when I wrote to Eckerd Drugs in Florida. But if I had given up after these two rejections, I wouldn't have found the success that lay just beyond.

Subsequently, I wrote a letter to Costco. (I'm relentless.) But this time the CEO personally called me and invited me to meet with him. Similar results happened later with Wal-Mart and Toys "R" Us, events that produced unpredictable breakthroughs.

Nobody likes being told no. It hurts. But if you keep asking, you'll eventually get a yes. And one great yes can heal a lot of minor wounds to our egos. Either way, no or yes, you'll never know unless you extend yourself.

REVEAL YOUR HAND

Always reveal the cards in your hand . . . at least to yourself. At all times, know what's going on in that head of yours. Develop an intimate relationship with the gremlins that batter your resolve and sabotage your game. Not that you want to hang out with them—they make lousy company—but so that you can recognize them and send them packing.

The Worrywart

Always on the lookout for trouble, this anxiety provoker is forever dredging up the worst possible scenario: *What if I look like an idiot? What if I flop? What if I end up like a bag lady?* This irrational thinking creates panic, diminishes power, and causes anxiety to spread quicker than a winter flu. Whenever I start worry~ ~y power away, I force myself to focus on the moment ~nd the task that is right in front of me. I literally talk to myself, saying things like: *I can handle this; I've managed this before, and I'll do it again.* And I don't stop until I believe my own words and am, once again, grounded in reality.

The Critic

A specialist in constant scrutiny and self-evaluation, this particularly nasty little gremlin is always there to point out your flaws and note your limitations. Ignoring your attributes, she creates anxiety by magnifying your liabilities. She's the one who is always saying that you should be other than you are . . . thinner, taller, smarter. The result of her presence is almost always decreased self-esteem.

The Sob Sister

Sob Sister, mournful little whiner that she is, takes you by the hand and leads you straight into the valley of depression with her feelings of hopelessness and victimization. For Sob Sister, everything is an obstacle or a barrier. Complaint and regret are her specialties. She is the voice that murmurs in your ear: *What's the point of trying?*

These rotten little tormentors are more than nuisances. If we allow them to, they'll rob us of our power, cause inertia, and blur our focus. They can so deplete our mental and emotional reserves that we are left empty and confused. All we want to do is curl up in a cave somewhere and take a long nap.

But it is action that banishes the Worrywart, slays the Critic, and knocks Sob Sister on her butt. It is by acting, by making mistakes, by falling on our faces and getting back in the game again, that we learn and grow.

NINE MOVES TO BANISH INERTIA

1. Write a letter to the editor of a trade publication or your local newspaper about an issue that concerns you.
2. Join an organization in which you can work with others to meet a common goal.

3. Serve on a board with people you'd like to get to know.
4. Write a note to your favorite author about a book you loved.
5. Make a phone call commending someone who gave you—or someone you know—special courtesy and attention.
6. Call about a college catalog and investigate a new area of creative interest.
7. Take a seminar to learn a new skill with people from other industries.
8. Turn down that side street you've never seen before; get to know the coworker on the other side of the hall, or the owner of the business next door.
9. Take a moment to look around and see how you can lend a hand, an arm, or a smile.

At some point you need to give up what's predictable for what's possible. Put one foot in front of the other and make your move.

Chapter 4

Create a Deliberate Journey

*"If you don't know where you're going,
any road will get you there."*

— ANONYMOUS

———————— ▬ ————————

Would you get into a taxi and tell the cabby, "Drive any-where"?

Would you wander onto the first plane you saw at the gate without bothering to ask where it's flying?

Of course not. Yet it's amazing how unfocused we can be about the biggest asset we have—our lives.

Goals shouldn't be blurry, half-baked, or fuzzy. Living a deliberate life requires being focused because today you're living out the choices you made yesterday, and tomorrow you will live out the choices you are making today.

The more precise, exact, streamlined, and specific you are about where you're going, the more powerful your life will be. It's like painting by numbers in reverse. First comes the big picture, then the bits that make the big picture complete.

But I don't mean you should wear blinders like the carriage horses in Central Park. They need them so they won't be spooked by traffic. But you *must* become aware of what's buzzing around you as you head toward your destination. You might want to follow a detour, or take a rest stop, or even make a 180-degree turn. Be focused, but also be flexible enough to bolt free and gallop down another path.

These side trips often yield unforeseen dividends.

Viagra was discovered when scientists were in the middle of a search for a new high blood pressure medicine. During clinical trials, patients kept reporting an interesting side effect—increased sexual arousal. By accident, the researchers had discovered something far more fascinating and profitable than what they'd originally been searching for. They shifted gears, abandoned the blood pressure route, and the rest is sexual history.

My early ambition was to be a lawyer, and it served me well. My dream kept me focused and striving, and eventually furnished the momentum I needed to escape the ghetto and move into the life I live today.

I've had a few other side trips along the way: pursuing a master's in public administration, trying to get into business school, becoming a fashion maven. None of these side trips ended up being my true vocation, but they enriched me, provided me with invaluable contacts, and revealed new and powerful directions.

The many years I spent working with some of the best designers and marketers in the world—Bill Blass, Oscar de la Renta, the Walt Disney Company, and Warner Brothers—were invaluable. It was during those years that I discovered my own creativity and developed my merchandising skills.

Now, nothing thrills or challenges me more than a blank canvas. I'm not only prepared for a world where products and solutions have to be created on the go, but I *thrive* on the challenge!

Living out your dream involves moving from one goal to another in a purposeful way. It is this focus that will open you up to the accidental discoveries that generate powerful breakthroughs and put the adventure back into life.

A GREAT ADVENTURE

<u>Do</u> Skip the Prepackaged Tour

You know what it's like when you put on someone else's glasses by mistake: You get an instant headache and the world is a blurry mess.

That's just what happens when you use someone else's vision as a guide for your own life.

Take a hard look at your goals. Do they invigorate you, or are they merely a reflection of what you think you *ought* to want?

Also, you need to ask yourself if this dream is something you still want. It is okay, even necessary, to put some goals aside from time to time. As we grow and change, as we gather new information, as the world around us evolves, we might find that a dream no longer serves us. There is no shame in abandoning a goal; sometimes that is the wisest course of action. You have the freedom to choose a destination; and you have the power to alter your plans.

For Mercedes Montealegre de Orjuela, the daughter of Colombian immigrants, fulfilling the American dream meant making money, and so she went at it with a vengeance.

The problem was, it wasn't *her* dream. But it took her a long while to discover that.

She dropped out of high school in the tenth grade, determined to get the things that other Americans had. She worked in a sewing factory, then a container factory, all the while keeping her eye on the prize of material success. Later, she found work at an insurance company and within six months had become a successful adjuster.

By 1985 she was prosperous, living the good life, complete with a spacious home and a Mercedes. But she wasn't happy; it wasn't enough. Having bought someone else's prepackaged tour, she was living someone else's dream of success.

So she gave it all up and shifted direction. After years of testing alternatives, she sold her luxury car and her home and embarked on pursuing a career in medicine.

This, no doubt, was a difficult choice. But now, many sleep-deprived nights later, Mercedes, age forty-one, is completing a medical residency in family practice.

Today, Dr. Mercedes Montealegre de Orjuela is married, a mother to Andres and six stepsons. She lives with her family in Florida in the very home she gave up to begin this journey.

Like Mercedes, you should choose a destination that energizes, challenges, and thrills *you*—not someone else. Otherwise, when the roadblocks show up—and they will—you'll lack the necessary power to move through them.

<u>Do</u> Narrow Your Focus

A deliberate life comes to fruition one set of goals at a time. You pour your complete intention in a specific direction and move with what unfolds.

When I was quite young and on the fast track in my career, I learned that my biological clock was ticking at double time. Endometriosis was ferociously damaging my plumbing, and I would soon be unable to have any children.

I had to refocus my attention and energy from the world of business to becoming a mother, even though it was a frantic interruption to my neatly planned out life. My husband, Steve, and I both really wanted children. And although we would have been happy to adopt a baby, we decided to exhaust the biological route first. We found the best infertility specialist in New York and got to work. Lots of drugs and several operations later, I delivered three sons, two years apart.

Even the most gifted women have to pick and choose. As we discussed before—and contrary to popular opinion—limited, finite human beings really *can't* "have it all."

Renee Fleming, an opera diva who is so popular that her concerts are sold out for years, surprisingly was once a jazz *and* opera singer. Over time, it became clear to her that she couldn't be on the road with a jazz band and train classically. She had to streamline her focus. And although she loves opera, she misses jazz. Today, she struggles with blending her traveling opera life and her role as a single mother.

<u>Do</u> Plan Your Own Itinerary

The wish for Prince Charming to come along and take her to his castle is a fantasy that even the most rebellious and successful woman might have lodged somewhere in the back of her mind.

Even with all my independence, I was no exception. When I started out, I didn't know what I wanted. I just knew what I *didn't* want: metal bars across my windows, roaches crawling into my ear at night, junkies on my doorstep.

I was sure of these things, but my ultimate destination wasn't so obvious. By the time I married my husband, at age twenty-four, I was exhausted from strategizing and fighting against what I didn't want. I just wanted some rest; I wanted someone else to be the decision maker in my life. Now I know that when I make decisions out of weakness or exhaustion or vulnerability, I often get hurt.

He was older and more experienced; I was crazy about him and knew he loved me. *Maybe he'll know where we're supposed to go, what we should do next,* I thought.

Here I was, the rebel of the family, the only girl who'd ever left home for a reason other than marriage, and I was still struggling to fit into the confining garments of my mother and aunts, who allowed the men in their lives or others to plan their destinies.

But soon those restrictive clothes began to chafe me.

I found myself sitting at the breakfast table, listening to my husband talk about his goals and dreams and thinking, *Are you just going to sit there and pretend you have nothing to add? Where do you want to go? How do you want to get there?* The problem was: I had few answers to my own questions.

I was a feisty young woman with dozens of ideas of my own. There was no reason for me to hang back and sit on the sidelines.

That yearning inside couldn't be filled by my husband's—or anyone else's—direction. I had to be my own decision maker. I had to design the unfolding of my own life.

Once I saw this, I loosened the strings of my old-fashioned corset and began to breathe deeply again.

<u>Do</u> Put Yourself First

Just like our grandmas, who were always the last to sit down at the dinner table, many of us wait until everyone else is satisfied before we pay attention to ourselves.

Pushing everyone else's needs ahead of our own is just another detour. It's another excuse to stay off course.

We must teach ourselves and others the importance of honoring our needs and desires.

Linda Novey White is a survivor, a woman who rose out of childhood poverty to become the CEO of an international consulting firm. Along the way she beat cancer three times, struggled through a divorce, and lived through the chronic illness of two daughters and the tragic death of her third.

While raising her three little girls, Linda discovered a way to teach them an important lesson about balance.

Each weekday around noon when the soap opera *As the World Turns* came on, the girls were given a rest period while their mom kicked back and relaxed. In the beginning the girls bitterly complained, "We're not tired now. We don't need a rest."

But Linda insisted, "Maybe *you* don't feel tired now, but *I* do. I need some quiet time alone so that I can be a nicer mommy this afternoon."

What does a little girl learn from such a statement? She is taught an essential lesson about tradeoffs and a woman's need for her own space and time. It's a lesson a girl can use herself one day and ultimately pass on to others.

In Linda Novey White's case, her daughters eventually grew so accustomed to these rest times that they became sleepy whenever they heard the soap opera theme song.

Linda says, "There is no reason to perpetuate the fantasy that we can fix it all, be it all, do it all twenty-four hours a day, seven days a week." We have to be honest with ourselves and others. We have to take responsibility for insisting on what we need to renew ourselves.

Now that Linda's kids are grown, she still makes sure she gives herself these special times.

"I work in a home office now, and it's hard to break away and take the breaks that one would in a regular office environment," she says. "Because I travel over two hundred days a year for business, it is even more difficult to find time just for me. I've adjusted by making some deals with myself."

Her "deals" include the following maxims:

- I don't work on airplanes. That's my time for reading mindless novels or magazines. It's my escape time.
- I take twenty-minute power naps once a day as often as possible. Sometimes these occur in public restrooms if there is no other place.
- I have ice cream or a candy bar when I've achieved small victories.
- In my home office, I sometimes don't take a shower until afternoon.
- I get a manicure (somewhere in the world) once or twice a month. You can't work and get a manicure at the same time, so it's enforced quiet time.
- When I'm really bone tired, I schedule a massage and/or a facial. This is my time to park my brain on "idle" or gain some "juice" for my depleted "batteries."

- ◆ On my most indulgent days, I take a book to the patio in the middle of the day and read for a while or simply daydream.

For Linda, daydreaming is a way to reflect on her goals, the wish list of things she'd like to do in the future.

"I'm going to take yoga lessons and do meditation and take ballet and archery lessons again someday, and I daydream about that," she says. "I am going to learn another language and take some more gourmet cooking classes. I'm going back to the gym and lose twenty pounds and quit skipping meals. All this is in my daydreams."

Linda has been fantasizing since she was a poor girl living in Tennessee. Back then she imagined flying on airplanes to faraway places, taking long hot baths without having to boil water on a stove. She daydreamed about having a new car that didn't always need to be repaired and of reading books whenever she wanted without having to go borrow them from the lady down the street.

These dreams were a way of giving herself permission to think about her own desires as well as the needs of others.

Now, as owner of her own business, she has made those fantasies, one by one, become realities.

The truth is, you can't *really* take good care of anyone else if you haven't tended to your own deep-seated needs and desires.

Try focusing on the *self* in the word *selfish* for a change.

Try treating yourself as if you're worth the special pampering and attention you give to others, because you *are* unique and wonderful . . . and if anybody deserves it, you do!

<u>Do</u> Stray off the Beaten Path

Being focused on your goal doesn't mean that you have to be blind to the jewels you might discover off your path.

Post-it notes were developed when scientists discovered a kind of glue they thought wasn't quite strong enough. Even though it had a nonpermanent stickiness, they found plenty of uses for it around the lab while they continued to focus on their real goal: a glue with a more permanent stick.

Then it dawned on them that if they found so many uses for it, so might others. Thus, the birth of Post-it notes.

While you're barreling down the road to your goal, keep alert for the surprises.

I was the reluctant entrepreneur. Even after I owned my own business, it still wasn't a real profession to me. Back in those days, being an entrepreneur wasn't as sexy as it is today. For a few years—even after some hard-won success and with a developing passion for business—I kept thinking that I was only doing this until I got to law school or business school and got a *real* job.

When I finally applied and didn't get into Harvard or Stanford, I was so heartbroken that I had a talk with one of the admissions counselors.

"You had an almost perfect verbal score, but your math needs improvement," the counselor told me. "You'll have to do some serious work if you want to get in."

Facing this choice made me focus.

Finally I was able to see that I was already where I needed to be. It felt too easy because it was so right.

In my case, I just had to see what was there in front of my nose.

<u>Do</u> Abandon a Dead End

If you come to a dead end, stop. Knowing when it's time to abandon a path is a necessary life skill.

I was hired away from my first big sales job by a competitor, a company owned by a man who became my father-in-law. Before I knew it, I'd become part of a close-knit Jewish family enterprise. I wasn't just the youngest female account executive, I was the *only* female account executive.

I wasn't the only Hispanic. I was just one of the few not on the factory floor, and the only one in the executive ranks. In the morning, I walked past the lines of tired-looking men and women, the very kind of people I had grown up with. I could feel their eyes on me as I clicked past them into my office, where I closed the door and tried—unsuccessfully—to shut them out.

I worked hard. I wanted to prove myself. I wanted to help this family—my new family—succeed. And as I kept discovering what was important to me, I realized there were certain things I would never get while I worked at the company.

The first was identity. There was a big chunk of me hiding out in the linen closet. I submerged the ambitious, playful, sassy part of myself in an attempt to impersonate an obedient drone. But the truth was, I didn't want to be just another worker bee in the hive; I wanted to be the queen. My real dream was to own a business, to call the shots and be the boss.

But in this company I was only a cog in a big machine. I had to hold my tongue and sit on my hands when we dealt with people I didn't respect.

I was so anxious to be accepted, to be a good wife, daughter-in-law, account executive, and mother, that I failed to focus on what was essential for my personal happiness.

This conflict took its toll. I felt under constant pressure. I cut back on sleep; I made sacrifices. Working in California, but with the home office based in New York, I often went in at six in the morning so I could speak to them at the start of business in their time zone and prove that I was a hard worker.

Often I left before the children were awake, missing those morning hellos. At other times, I dropped off my sons at childcare and cried all the way to the car, my two-year-old's wails still echoing in my head. In the parking lot, I would wipe the mascara from my cheeks and cover up the smudges under my eyes.

Who was this woman in the rearview mirror? What was I doing? Who was I doing it for? Was it making me happy?

Then a senior executive joined the firm. We had an opposing set of values, and coping with those differences grew harder and harder.

One day, when I suggested that we give a project to one of the young women in the office, he said derisively, "You can't get a Puerto Rican to do that." I sat in silence throughout the rest of the meeting, but I felt as if I were on fire.

That night, as I watched my sons crawling on the carpet playing with their Legos, his words kept ringing in my ears: *You can't get a Puerto Rican to do that . . . you can't get a Puerto Rican . . .*

I realized that one day my kids were going to look at me and decide whether or not they respected me based on how I'd lived my life.

I faced it: I was compromising myself by trying to be

part of this business. I was prostituting myself for money. I was playing out someone else's dream and story. No amount of money was worth that.

When I looked in the mirror, I felt that my real self was melting away like a snowwoman.

I wanted to work in an environment where every person was honored, where the assumption was that everyone has the capacity for greatness. But I thought my desire to design a company based on my own ethics and standards was too big for someone like me.

I hadn't given myself permission to dream that big, to want that much. So I gave myself permission to be miserable instead.

But I started to listen to my disappointment, my hurt, my rage, and the angst lit the way. Seeing myself through my children's eyes did the trick. Focusing on the mother I needed to be for them prodded me in the right direction. I began to consider all kinds of possibilities I hadn't entertained before.

I said to myself, *So what if I have two babies to take care of? I'll make the money in a different way.* And I started to look for how.

I went to my father-in-law, a kind and savvy businessman, and told him about a deal I wanted us to go after.

"It's a great situation," I began.

He listened to my presentation, but then he shook his head. "We can't do that," he replied, and turned back to his paperwork. When I didn't leave, he looked back up at me.

"Do you mind if I try?"

I saw the surprise pass over his face. Then he shrugged his shoulders and said, "Go ahead."

I could tell he didn't believe I could. Or would.

But I did.

In order to strike this deal on my own I had to gather together every scrap of belief in myself. It helped lots that my husband, who worked alongside me, encouraged me to try my crazy ideas. I had to delve into my center, where I'd kept the flame of my dream burning all those years. I had to focus clearly on the kind of life I knew was possible for me and my family. Then I had to break down my dream into steps and propel myself toward them.

First I did the research. Then I made the phone calls and set up a meeting. And before I knew it I was standing in an office shaking a buyer's hand.

I closed the deal on my own.

And then I resigned.

When I quit, employees in the company approached me and said, "Do you know what you're walking away from? Your husband is due to inherit this business."

And I said, "Number one, it's not my money. And number two, I can't compromise myself anymore."

I literally couldn't breathe.

It was a tough lesson in the importance of focus. But it was worth it.

TIPS FROM A FELLOW TRAVELER

Most of us have an intuitive sense of what we really want, but we allow it to remain vague and unclaimed, gathering dust on the shelf.

You might wander around saying, "I'd like to see China someday" or "I always thought I'd be a good painter." Yet without picking a clear destination, chances are the only con-nection you're going to have with China is your local takeout. And the only painting you're going to get done is your nails.

Be Specific

This small but powerful act brings your dreams out of the clouds and into reality. Pick a point in time three to five years from now. Imagine having created your ideal circum-stances. List your age and the ages of your children or signif-icant other. Where are you? What are you doing? Clearly state your destination. After filling out this picture, decide what you must put into play right now to make that picture an achievable goal.

Break It Down

What are the specific results you must achieve on your way toward this goal? I list my six-month, one-year, three-year, five-year, and ten-year goals and read them daily, before the day gets going. I even write the names of the peo-ple I intend to meet in each time period. Anyone I might need three years from now, I've got to get to know now.

Set the Pace

How will you know you're making progress? What are the landmarks, milestones along the way? By what date will you do x? When are you leaving, when do you arrive? If it's time for a U-turn, how will you know that?

Know What's in Your Gear

Popular psychology has a lot to say about the "baggage" we all carry around. But it's important for you to realize that some things you packed yourself, while others have crept into your baggage on their own.

On a recent trip, as I was getting my bag out of the car, I noticed a big bulge, but figured the contents had shifted around as I was driving to the airport. Of course, when I got to the plane my bag didn't fit in the overhead compartment. As I unzipped it to see what I could remove, out fell a big brown teddy bear. Unbeknownst to me, my son Andrew had sent along his teddy for good luck at what I had explained to him would be a tough presentation.

Not only did Mr. Willy come along on that trip but so did a frightened nine-year-old Debbie. At times like these I often have to remind her that she is safe, that all is well and we will be all right.

Your past is with you in the present. Keep building your awareness.

What serves you, and what doesn't? Are you bringing something to this journey you'd rather leave behind?

Give Up Control

Let go. Don't walk around expecting things to go your way. You can't control the outcome. It will rain, the attraction you came to see might be flooded out, your hotel might be struck by lightning.

Be led by a goal, but be rigorously flexible about pursuing it. It must be free of expectation.

With all my best-laid plans, it took me ten years and four colleges to get a bachelor's degree. When I finally attended commencement, I did so with a five-month-old snuggling close to me under my gown.

Another lesson came when I was attending a very important conference held by one of the most powerful trade organizations in my industry—the International Mass Retail Association (IMRA). The place was crawling with CEOs and the top-level decision makers from the most significant accounts in the country.

As usual, I had left nothing to chance. It took months to secure a great booth location, schedule meaningful meetings, and orchestrate the right seat between the right people at the right table for the closing dinner event. And if that wasn't enough, the entertainment that night would be Patti LaBelle, one of my favorite divas.

Just as I was about to change into my fancy dress for the evening, I got a phone call in my hotel room. My brother's heart had stopped, and he was in a coma.

When I arrived at the intensive care unit my cockiness evaporated. I was humbled by all that was out of my hands and out of my control. No planning, no orchestrating, no *anything* could change what mattered most.

Beware Detour Ahead

There's always a detour ahead. Sometimes it'll lead us to exciting heights, where we feel like we're on top of the world. And sometimes these intriguing new trails end in failed expeditions.

Those grinning skeletons lying along the path aren't

much comfort; misery doesn't care much about company on one of these seemingly fruitless climbs.

But even though detours are inevitable, they don't need to be frustrating exercises in futility. We can learn a lot along the way . . . including how to get back on course.

Envy

Envy is a discontent fueled by a painful desire for someone else's advantage, and it keeps us looking over our shoulder at what everyone else has. Instead of begrudging another woman's success, notice what draws you to her, what piques your interest, what turns your head. Where do *you* find beauty?

Don't just throw daggers at Martha Stewart; listen to what your envy is trying to tell you. What's she got that grabs your attention? Her empire, the know-how to make perfect lemon squares, her independence, the power to do it her way? Once you figure it out, start pinpointing the moves you can make *today* to head in one of these directions.

Used this way, envy can shine a light on your path.

Guilt

Are you hanging on the side of a cliff, looking back down at the dizzying heights you've already climbed, commiserating about whether you chose the right footholds? Maybe you made some stupid choices along the way. Maybe you kicked gravel in another climber's face, and you're consumed with guilt.

But guilt isn't a virtue. There's no positive payoff for sitting around feeling miserable, except the chance to sit on your duff for a while. Guilt can serve as a signpost along the way, letting us know that we have unfinished business from the past, or perhaps we should be doing something differently in the present . . . or maybe we just need to take a refreshing break.

If you need a rest, take one. Make amends wherever necessary and possible, note the lessons learned, and vow to choose more carefully in the future.

Then get on with it—because as long as you're looking backward you can't focus on the climb above.

Revenge

There was a time in my life when my own path took an unfortunate detour. I wasted part of every day plotting revenge against someone who'd hurt me. I was always thinking about how I could get back at her or sabotage her business. It got so bad that I even imagined her hurt or dead. But I finally noticed that all my plotting revenge and retribution left little time to focus on my own goals. I was having difficulty getting anything accomplished; my head was as cluttered as my desk.

I knew I needed to move on in order to free up my energy.

One day I gave myself a goal: to give up my bitterness for just one day. And that felt so good that I extended it for another. And soon I had let it go for good.

As soon as I stepped into a space of forgiveness, the heavens opened, my creativity flowed, and I had the energy to continue my climb.

Not all detours are a waste of time and energy. Whether we've gotten sidetracked by envy, guilt or the desire for revenge, we can use the detour to illuminate, guide, and fuel our way back onto our main path. And we can bring along the valuable lessons we learned on those roads less traveled.

Feeling Lost?

Maybe you haven't taken any of those particular detours, but you're feeling stuck or stymied. Are you wandering in circles, spinning your wheels, unable to get anything done? I've found these actions are mind-clearers that can help defog my view and get me moving again.

Clean House

Yes, I mean your closets full of clothes that don't fit you and remind you how skinny you used to be; the shoes you haven't worn in five years; the junk in your basement, your files; the ancient cosmetics and toiletries you're stashing under the bathroom sink . . . your relationships.

Is there someone you need to apologize to? Is there someone you need to forgive? Is there someone you need to remove from your life?

Make a list of all the nasty little messes you have lying around and start eliminating them one at a time. These forms of pollution are clogging up the flow of your life energy, energy you need to power your dream.

Indulge Yourself

Stop running. When was the last time you did something for you . . . a manicure, a massage, a nice hot bath, a restful cup of herbal tea? When was the last time you let yourself wonder, speculate, ruminate?

Lighten Up

Have mercy. Don't take yourself so seriously, and remember we live one here and now at a time. Step outside of yourself and see your place in history, in the human chain, in evolution, in the universe. I keep a universe ball around just to remind me of the nanosecond I occupy in the continuum of time.

Take a Walk on the Wild Side

Do something fun. Go dancing, have a picnic, belt out a tune. Put yourself in a completely different, no-stress environment. I love going to my son's basketball games. I get to scream, jump up and down, and act silly. I also get to be dumb, because someone usually has to explain to me why the referee just did what he did.

Get Immediate Gratification

Some of the projects I'm working on are very long-term; some won't even be accomplished in my lifetime. So, I often create mini-projects that I can accomplish easily and "see" to completion in a short amount of time.

When I'm looking for a quick fix, I usually end up at

one of my favorite places, Home Depot—I'm the queen of "do-it-yourself" home improvement projects. Recently, I went doorknob crazy. I bought some beautiful brass handles and replaced twenty-eight of them.

And every time I feel the cool, heavy metal as I open a door, I get happy.

THE SIXTY-MINUTE FOCUS MAKEOVER

The makeovers I'm talking about aren't the ones you find in women's magazines or beauty parlors.

I had one of those myself when I was in high school, heading off for my junior class dance. After a four-hour blitz, I staggered out with a masklike complexion perfect for a Kabuki dancer, artificial nails so long and curved that I could barely open my wallet, and a pile of such elevated curls that it was hard to sit up straight in the backseat of my friend's car.

It was a makeover all right; and I spent the rest of the day frantically undoing it.

It's tempting to go for these exterior makeovers in the wild hope that they'll really change us. But deep down we realize how fleeting and superficial these types of changes are.

The makeovers I'm talking about are focused on your interior and are aimed at building your inner strength and resources.

Most of us have at least three things we've been meaning to do—sometimes for ages. Write them down on a piece of paper and tape them to your morning mirror so you see them every day.

Now carve out sixty minutes per week to take action on one of these. (Ten minutes per day equals sixty minutes per week, leaving one day off. This is time you spend talking to supermarket checkout cashiers, shooting the breeze about the weather, being "nice" to a coworker or employee.) The several hours I carved out of my depression to fill out an award application changed my life.

Chapter 5

Fuel Your Dream

"There are hearts and hands always ready to make generous intentions become noble deeds."
—HELEN KELLER

━━━━━━━━━━━━━━━━━━━ ■ ━━━━━━━━━━━━━━━━━━━

This is no time to be on a diet. I want you to create a sumptuous buffet of the best, most inspiring, tantalizing, luscious people you can find. They should be:

- People who expand your ideas about what's possible.
- People so compelling and inviting that they call you to greatness.
- People who challenge you to be better than you imagine yourself to be.

Think of it as an all-you-can-eat smorgasbord where you fill up your plate and can keep coming back for more.

You don't have to personally know your role models:

Oprah, Amelia Earhart, the woman down the street who went to law school at fifty . . . it doesn't matter who these remarkable people are as long as they nourish you and fuel your journey.

Role models provide a great opportunity to learn about yourself and expand your own experience. Whether your role model is Marie Curie, Isabel Allende, or Tina Turner, you can rummage through the bins of your heroine's experience and pick the life lessons you need.

Today there is a cornucopia of highly visible female role models. But it hasn't always been easy to find smart, ambitious women who embody the positive qualities you might want to emulate.

I felt this lack when I was a struggling young mother trying to reconcile my role as a mom and my drive to create. I yearned for a female entrepreneur with a family to whom I could look for inspiration and guidance. I had so many questions:

- How did she play the roles of mother, business-woman, wife and/or lover, and activist and not suffer an identity crisis?
- How did she convince herself that she *could* achieve her goals, that she deserved success?
- How did she keep her eye on the prize while bandaging soccer wounds and refereeing sibling squabbles?

But there was no one for me to talk to or even read about. Most of the women around me were primarily interested in cooking, laundry, and decorating their homes. And

although I had to do these things, too, my passion was business—competition, closing deals, growing the bottom line—
an arena largely inhabited by men.

I'm glad to say that's not true anymore.

As a girl growing up poor in the South Bronx, I wasn't
sure *what* success looked like, but I was pretty sure it didn't
look like me. There was no chubby, freckled, bespectacled
Puerto Rican girl in any movie I'd ever seen or any book I'd
ever read. I'd never heard of an Hispanic female CEO or
scholar.

The women I saw were worn-out domestics and shop
clerks, carrying groceries to their walk-ups, trying to summon the energy to make it through the day.

I saw no Hispanic spitfire, brainy and bossy, making
serious money, having fun.

So if I couldn't find a role model, who was I supposed to
follow? How do you find your own path and manage to stay
on it until you reach your destination without positive
images illuminating the way?

A BIT OF THIS . . . A BIT OF THAT

Without realizing what I was doing, I began stitching together a mental model for myself, constructed from the qualities of those around me. Using that woman's straight back,
this one's warm and patient smile, another's coolly controlled
temper, I created a kind of rag doll I kept by my side.

And once I began sewing, I saw that I had more positive
images than I realized. The women around me might not
have been running corporations, but they had plenty of
qualities to admire.

One of these special ladies was my gorgeous seventh grade teacher, Miss Lamb. With a Halle Berry cocoa-brown complexion, she was the most beautiful woman I'd ever seen in person. As an awkward young girl, waiting to blossom, I admired the way she glided across a room, the way she held a fork. She was elegant and poised, smart and sexy, warm and caring, all at the same time. This was a powerful combination. I'd never known that a woman could embody all these qualities at once.

Then there was my Titi (aunt) Angela,* who lived on the Lower East Side of New York City where I often escaped on the weekends.

Titi Angela was a single mother, struggling to support my cousins in a public housing project so bleak that I had to straddle puddles of urine while riding up in the elevator.

But her tenement surroundings didn't seem to matter. Inside her cinder block apartment, she had built a peaceful nest, fragrant with her home-cooked meals and permeated with love. She made me feel safe in the midst of a world of drug addicts and crime.

What was happening *inside* her apartment was far more powerful than the poverty lurking outside. I watched her perform her everyday magic the same way I watched her make cookies: taking the little she had and turning it into gold.

Flora Davidson was my tough-minded political science professor at Barnard College. She was tall, strong, and very pregnant, and I remember visiting her office after her baby was born, seeing her daughter in a crib by her side, happily napping while the professor worked on her notes. This

---

*Not her real name.

image made a profound impression on me. I considered for the first time how I might structure my own life to integrate children and career.

As my thesis adviser, Professor Davidson taught me a lesson that has remained with me all my life. The day I handed in the first draft of my thesis concerning the plight of undocumented Mexican laborers in the United States, I was recovering from a C-section and in the middle of planning a move to California. I dragged myself into her office with milk leaking down my blouse, exhausted, and forty pounds overweight.

I'd written my thesis during stolen moments between breast feedings and diaper changes, and I believed it was one of the best papers I'd ever written.

Professor Davidson didn't agree.

I sat listening in disbelief as we reviewed the pages she had ripped apart, deleting whole paragraphs with a red pen.

"You should expand this. That isn't clear. Give me some examples."

I tried to hold back my tears, but I couldn't. With each turning page, my confidence crumbled.

"You'll pass with this," she finished at last, "but I know you can do better."

I cried so hard that the mascara ran down my face in lanes.

"You don't understand," I told her. "I don't have anything more to give."

She didn't flinch. "You can use this as an opportunity to discover what you're really made of, or you can settle for what you already know you are."

I left her office confused, bewildered, my head spinning

with questions. *How could she have criticized my work so severely? What does she want from me? How much more can a human possibly do?*

When I got home, I collapsed. I had no intention of ever looking at that paper again.

But then it began calling out to me. It was a little voice that wouldn't go away.

"C'mon, Deborah," it said. "Look one more time. See what you can do!"

I put my excuses aside and took one more look at the paper. I saw that the professor had been right: There *was* more I could do.

In the middle of the night I woke with new ideas. The next morning I went to the library and dug deeper into my research. I found myself kicking through imaginary walls into rooms I'd never entered. It was such a revelation to discover that I had more to offer, much more!

Professor Davidson gave me an A– on my revision, a big deal from her. But from that day on, I was ruined for mediocrity. I'd experienced the thrill of discovery. I'd acquired a taste for excellence, and I've never lost it.

And then there was my mother.

As a girl, I was ashamed of my parents. I was embarrassed by their dark skin, their Spanish accents, and their polyester clothes—and mostly by their respectful manner in the presence of people who treated them like second-class citizens—or downright garbage. I didn't even want to be seen with them, and I crossed the street rather than walk by their sides.

Yet for all her problems, my mother was the heroine of our neighborhood, able to operate much better in the outside world than inside her home. She was always leading rent strikes and finding creative ways to help people in need.

One Christmas, I realized what tough stuff she was made of.

Every year the Methodist church where my father was a minister in the South Bronx collected toys at Christmas. The kids in our neighborhood were so poor that one of these toys was often the only gift they received. The church was their Santa Claus.

One year the church's request to the Marine Corps for gifts was apparently misplaced. It was only a few days before Christmas and there we were without a single doll or stuffed animal, and a whole neighborhood of kids about to be disappointed.

Someone else might have thrown up her hands in defeat, but not my mother. To her, the problem wasn't a community crisis but an opportunity.

She called a local radio station and made a heartfelt appeal live on the air, asking New Yorkers to come to the aid of kids who had so little in their lives.

I'll never forget the response.

Within hours, people from all over the city began to arrive. I stood at my window watching as brawny construction workers and secretaries appeared with their arms full of toys. Trucks and taxis and bikes were double-parked in front of the church. There was an unbelievable outpouring of gifts—and it continued even after the holidays were over.

Through her own personal power, my mother had mobilized that tidal wave of generosity . . . a flood of kindness that blessed the givers as well as the recipients.

My mother had many public moments like this, moments when she appeared powerful, sane, and strong. But privately, behind the closed doors of our family life, there were many more times when she was weak, vulnerable, and depressed. She might have been able to organize rent strikes, but she seemed unable to control her own inner chaos.

My mother was a cautionary image of what could happen if I gave up on my dreams. A near genius with an IQ of 158, she never made it to medical school, her saddest regret. Assaulted by a world where she was only a woman and a "spic," she acquiesced, first to her father's expectations and later to her husband's.

For years this seemingly peaceful resignation would surface in the form of violent rages and debilitating bouts of sadness. Compromising her deepest desires had exacted a terrible toll on her; she often sank into such a listless depression that I'd leave her in a rocking chair in the morning and return from school to find her in the exact same position, still in her robe. It was frightening to witness her inability to direct her energy for herself.

I promised myself this would never happen to me. I was willing to pay the cost of success, but the price of dreams unfulfilled was simply too high.

One of my most important role models, especially in my early years, was the first love of my life, Miguel.* It didn't matter that he was a boy. He was from my world, and he was a powerful catalyst in changing how I looked at my future.

When I was fourteen, and going into my junior year in high school, my father took charge of a new church, and I transferred to Yonkers High School. It was there that I first saw Miguel.

*Not his real name.

He was gorgeous: six feet tall with raven hair and the long, lean body of a track star. I had just emerged from my adolescent chubbiness, and I could hardly believe that he noticed me.

Miguel knew what it was like to grow up with low expectations, in an atmosphere of poverty and dread.

Soon he would understand me better than anyone.

He might have come from my world, but he already had a foot firmly planted outside of it. He *knew* he was going to excel. He'd set his sights on getting into Harvard, and *nothing* was going to stop him.

He'd been on this track since elementary school. As part of a special inner-city program for gifted children, he'd won a four-year scholarship to the Hackley School for boys, an exclusive prep school in Tarrytown, New York.

Miguel lived at school during the week, but he came home on the weekends, when we would study together. I noticed how much more advanced his work was than mine. He was grappling with philosophy and calculus, while I was answering easy social studies questions. He was preparing himself for an Ivy League future, while it seemed that I was just wandering in scholastic mediocrity.

Seeing Miguel aim so high made me adjust my own sights. I knew I was going to attend college, but *where* I was going had never been an issue. Maybe a local school—I wasn't sure. But Miguel *did* know where he was headed.

I saw that if I wanted to attend a prestigious college I'd have to catch up with applicants like Miguel. I'd have to improve my English and study harder than I ever had before.

So I developed a system. Each night, after I completed my own high school work, I also began doing Miguel's. I absorbed everything he brought home.

We studied for our SATs together. We quizzed each other on differential equations, Isaac Newton, the theory of relativity. It was great to have the companionship, and it was even greater to know I was creating a real chance at a whole new life.

I was expanded by the riches Miguel brought into our cramped living room every Saturday afternoon when we studied Shakespeare and Latin, and on Saturday nights when he taught me about my body and the range of my heart.

By the time I was ready to apply to college, my whole perspective had widened. I wanted to prove that I could excel at the highest levels. I realized that where I went to college would be vital in determining my eventual place in the world.

Thanks to Miguel, I raised my sights. I visited several minority open house weekends at Ivy League schools and decided to apply. For months, we worked hard collecting letters of recommendation and rewriting essays.

Miguel got accepted to Harvard and would later graduate summa cum laude.

And one day I reached into our rusty mailbox and found a miracle—a letter announcing I had been accepted into Wellesley with a full scholarship.

That's what role models are.

They challenge us to reach higher by the sheer power of who they are.

SPICING UP THE SPREAD

A powerful woman can be your role model without her knowledge or permission.

But a mentor is an *active* participant in your life, someone who agrees to be your advocate. A mentor counsels you, introduces you to people, keeps you moving in the right direction.

Having a trusted advocate is one of the smartest ways to grow your career—and your life.

Some of us are lucky to have one close at hand.

In Barbara Corcoran's case, her mother acted as her advocate during her early years—and it saved her.

Corcoran, known as the Queen of New York Real Estate, is the chairman and founder of Manhattan's largest privately owned real estate firm. She runs one of the most successful luxury real estate firms in the world.

All her life, Corcoran was dyslexic, but she didn't know it.

All she knew was that she had difficulty keeping up in school.

All she knew was that she was considered stupid, that she didn't have friends, that she was the last to be picked for games.

But when she got home each night she found a loving mother who didn't care about any of this.

When she walked in the door with her low grades or her bruised feelings, her mother said, "Forget school. I say you're wonderful. I think you're perfect exactly the way you are."

This unconditional love and her mother's unwavering belief in her negated everything that happened in Barbara's school day.

Now a phenomenally successful woman known for her accessibility as a manager, Corcoran still remembers being a rejected child who had only one person rooting for her.

And that one person was all she needed.

We all need trusted people who believe in us and support our ambitions. When the going gets tough—and it will—we need to have someone out there, supporting us and our causes, reminding us of our greatness.

KEEP ON THE LOOKOUT

You never know where help or encouragement might come from.

Don't assume just because someone is high ranking—or male—that he won't be willing to help you.

That's a lesson I learned with Jim Sinegal, the CEO of Costco.

Although I'd been a vendor to Costco for several years, I was able to place only small orders here and there. I couldn't seem to get to first base on the big programs. This was frustrating because I kept noticing an umbrella program at Costco that I knew I could produce better, at a lower price, if I only had the chance. But there was a long-time vendor blocking my access and a whole line of buyers who were satisfied with their program. They weren't exactly dying to hear my ideas and plans.

I knew attacking my competitor was futile, so what could I do? Hang around headquarters in my best suit, waiting to be noticed? Keep pounding on doors that appeared permanently sealed shut?

I was too eager, determined, and ambitious for any of that.

I wanted to maneuver myself to the big buffet, not the

little side tables with the hors d'oeuvres. So I decided to look for a way that I could be of value to Costco, other than selling them merchandise. (And no, I can't tell you what it was.) When I found it, I wrote directly to their CEO, Jim Sinegal, introducing myself, offering him my help, and asking him for his. To my delight, he responded, offering an attentive ear, encouraging hand, and solid advice.

That beginning eventually allowed me to present my case to Costco and negotiate a test program. We did create the best rain umbrella value in the country. By the following year, we had grown the business by 61 percent, and we've continued to build a mutually profitable relationship.

Just as important, Jim Sinegal has proven to be a great long-term supporter of mine in the often-bruising corporate world. He has taken the time to congratulate me when I've won an award or give me advice when I feel like I'm in over my head.

When I doubt myself, or think I'm aiming too high, it is a powerful boost to remember that someone who's been on the cover of *Forbes* and runs a $27 billion business thinks I'm capable of succeeding.

Never underestimate the amount of goodwill in the world, even among people you think are too high ranking to notice you. Most successful business people have struggled up the ladder themselves. They're often pleased to be asked for help or advice. And chances are they'll admire your spunk and ambition because these are traits they've cultivated themselves.

So go ahead: Reach out—and up!

BORROW A RECIPE OR TWO

With an eye on your *current goals,* look around for someone who possesses the know-how you seek, then ask if he or she would be willing to act as your mentor. I've done this a number of times in my career, and I've never regretted it.

Don't allow your fear to keep you from taking this important life step. You might be refused, but even if you are, your heart will heal. And you might be surprised at the response you receive. In my experience, each mentor was flattered that I asked, and each offered me hard-won wisdom I could have never found in a book.

Here's how to get a yes.

- *Know what's in it for them.* Make sure you clearly see, from their point of view, what they get out of the deal. Although it doesn't have to be monetary, they should receive some sort of reward for their efforts on your behalf.
- *Share your blueprint.* Be able to describe your game plan and their potential role in a few sentences or less. No matter how complex, every well-constructed plan can be explained in a concise, pithy manner.
- *Make a specific request.* Suggest a specific amount of input, at so many intervals, to be completed in a certain period of time.
- *Get a referral.* If they can't fulfill your request, ask them for the name of someone who might.
- *Be a good student.* A good mentor is part fan club and part peanut gallery. Be ready for both.

A NOTE ON COACHING

Do keep in mind that, depending on what you're trying to accomplish, it might be time to call in additional help. In the Little League, a volunteer coach works fine. But when you're playing a major-league game, only a pro will do.

As in sports, there are coaches for everything: voice, public speaking, negotiating, sales. Don't hire a tennis coach to work on your jump shot. Make sure you hire a coach with competence in the area where you need help.

I've enlisted the guidance of professional coaches throughout my career, and the results have been invaluable.

SHARE THE GOODIES

As every good host knows, there's nothing more satisfying than watching your guests enjoy a great spread.

Mentoring works the same way. Except that you'll get more than the pure joy generosity creates. Sharing what you've learned and experienced gives you an opportunity to make a difference in someone's life *and* yours. This two-way process will give you more access to:

- ◆ Your own gifts
- ◆ Your own lessons
- ◆ Your own capacity to grow

But, rewards and benefits aside, it doesn't matter *why* we give, as long as we do it.

Extend that Hand

Look around you. It's not your textbook learning that matters—it's your *story;* it's the way you've met your challenges, survived, and triumphed. Who could use your life lessons, your encouragement? Who would you find more fulfilling to work with?

- ◆ Infants
- ◆ Children
- ◆ High school kids
- ◆ College students
- ◆ Adults
- ◆ Elderly people
- ◆ Physically challenged people
- ◆ Learning disabled people
- ◆ New moms
- ◆ Parents

What issues call you to action?

- ◆ Education
- ◆ Environment
- ◆ Health care
- ◆ Racial equality
- ◆ Literacy
- ◆ Peace
- ◆ Hunger
- ◆ Politics
- ◆ Spirituality
- ◆ Artistic creativity

NO TIME LIKE THE PRESENT

Some of you might be thinking that you're not ready now. You have no particular expertise; you have nothing to share, nothing to give. Maybe you're running on empty and are waiting to get replenished first.

But these are precisely the times when we must share what we think we don't have. And if you're reading this book you definitely have something to share; at a minimum you could work on a literacy project.

As with developing a regular exercise program, it's easy to give in to lethargy. You have no energy, so you don't exercise. But you won't get the energy back until you do. Stepping out will refuel you in ways you could never predict.

Often, when I'm most depleted, I nibble on the nourishing memories of time spent mentoring others. It's been particularly gratifying for me to share my story with the girls at Taft High School. I remember how it felt to live isolated from the loops of politics, commerce, and power. Now, when I return to Taft, I know those girls can't always see the possibilities in themselves, so for a few moments I try to hold the hope for them. I represent tangible proof that it's possible to bridge the river between poverty and success. In their eyes, I can see the same hunger I once had.

One of the greatest benefits I've received from mentoring is a feeling of humble gratitude. When I teach others, I hear in my own words the sage advice that was given so freely to me by generous, loving people. I've come so far only because so many have helped me. These people were teachers who taught for the sheer joy of sharing their passion, without expecting anything in return. The best I can do is honor their example—and move the gift along.

Oseola McCarty, an elderly washerwoman who died in 1999 at the age of ninety-one, has become a model for selfless giving.

McCarty, who did not even know what the word *philanthropy* meant, decided to give away her life savings of $150,000 after she was diagnosed with cancer. She endowed a scholarship for poor students in her home state of Mississippi, donating everything she had to help some stranger receive a college education.

An only child who outlived her family, McCarty lived a solitary existence surrounded by piles of clothes she washed and ironed for others. After giving her gift, her lifetime of loneliness changed abruptly as the world showered her with accolades. But the humble lady didn't want monuments or proclamations.

On the occasion of her endowment she said simply, "I'm giving it away so that the children won't have to work so hard, like I did."

McCarty left more than money; her greatest gift was her example of selfless giving. After hearing of her sacrifice, Ted Turner, the multibillionaire, was inspired to give away a billion dollars himself to the cause of education. And contributions from more than six hundred donors have been added to McCarty's original scholarship.

"There's a lot of talk about self-esteem these days," she said once. "It seems pretty basic to me. If you want to feel proud of yourself, you've got to do things you can be proud of. *Feelings follow actions.*"

You may not have $150,000 to share, like Oseola, but you can still make a powerful impact on another person's life.

There are many ways, and here's one.

Count Me In is a nonprofit organization dedicated to

women's economic independence. One five dollar contribution at a time, they are working to create a $25 million national loan fund for women. The money will then be redistributed in the form of small-business loans and scholarships ranging from $500 to $10,000.

And whether you are the giver or the recipient, you'll know that women pooled together to help someone's dream come to life.

Never underestimate the force of one small act to move and inspire others. And remember, every time you make a difference for someone else you gain greater access to your own power.

NINE ENERGIZING TREATS

1. **List** three people who have made a difference in your life. For each person, finish the following statement: I am grateful to you because . . .
2. **Write** a note to someone from this list and thank that person for all he or she has done for you. Describe how different your life is today because of this person. It doesn't matter if you mail this note or not.
3. **Go** to a card shop and read the cards in the encouragement section. Find one that really touches you and mail it to yourself.
4. **Document** some of your accomplishments. If you think you don't have any, start with skills you might have taken for granted: learned to read, learned to write, learned to swim . . .

5. **Form** a mutual admiration group. People it with friends who have experienced some of your greatness and will remind you of it when you need it.

6. **Pay** for someone else. When I'm at a toll booth, sometimes I pay the toll for the person behind me. All day I know someone is telling the story of the crazy lady who paid the toll for a complete stranger.

7. **Assemble** photos of women you admire. Keep them on your desk, your dresser, or the bathroom sink to remind you of what is possible.

8. **Share** your successes. Celebrate your accomplishments, even the simple ones, with those you love. Acknowledge accomplishments, yours and theirs, with simple pleasures: an ice cream sundae, a trip to a park, a new dress . . .

9. **Savor** your victories. Create a victory wall. Paper it with letters, photos, articles, anything that reminds you of how special, how wonderfully unique, you really are!

Chapter 6

Take Something or Somebody On

"Every action we take, everything we do, is either a victory or defeat in the struggle to become what we want to be."

— ANNE BYRHHE

Fighting is necessary. There's no winning without it.

Whether you pick a fight or a fight picks you, you need to know how to "float like a butterfly and sting like a bee."

That doesn't mean you have to be out there swinging at everything that pisses you off. Engaging in battle should be a strategic move, not an impulsive reaction because you've lost your cool or are having an emotional upheaval.

Given that most of us don't have the physical prowess of Muhammad Ali's daughter, Laila, or the magical powers of Xena the Warrior Princess, we need to face off in new and powerful ways.

With practice, you can develop your own discipline and skill, your own strength and grace in the ring.

And you can win.

STAND UP FOR YOURSELF

I learned a lot about fighting from watching my mother.

She was a scrappy little bantamweight who became a fury whenever she witnessed some grave injustice.

But when it came to her own needs, she was stuck on the sidelines, often too immobilized by depression to change out of her robe or even wash her hair.

As a child, I wondered why she couldn't be as assertive in protecting herself as she was when protecting other people. What good were all her defensive moves if she couldn't use them on her own behalf?

Watching her, I decided that the first person I would learn to stand up for was *myself.*

From the day I was knocked down as a kindergartner in that Harlem elementary school, I knew I was going to have to battle for my survival.

But I wasn't stupid.

I knew I couldn't overpower the girls whose favorite lunch period recreation was shoving my face in the dirt. I couldn't spar with the bullies who chased me down muddy, garbage-strewn alleys and snatched my lunch on the way to school.

So I learned to develop my own killer moves, strategies of assertiveness, perseverance, offensive sparring, and even the occasional retreat. This early training served me well when I moved from the mean streets of the inner city into the tough world of business.

STEP INTO THE RING

Near the end of my junior year, I went to the guidance counselor at Yonkers High School and asked her to send my transcripts to Wellesley and several other prestigious colleges. I gave her a list of schools in which I was interested.

She raised an eyebrow, then pushed the paper back across the desk to me.

"Stop kidding yourself, Deborah. You're a bright girl, but you'll never get into those places," she said. "You're better off aiming for a two-year community college. Maybe try for a career as a legal secretary."

"But that's not what I want."

She gave me an exasperated look. "Listen, you're not going to get in, okay? And it's a waste of my time and the school's resources to process your transcripts and send them out for nothing."

I had been told no plenty of times, but I'd never been blindsided like this.

I snatched my list off her desk and stormed out of her office.

With Miguel as a guide, I'd begun my climb out of the inner city. The first rung on my ladder was to be a college education; the top rung would be a career in law.

And in less than three minutes on this October morning, that misguided "guidance" counselor had tried to yank the ladder out from under me before I had even begun to climb.

She thought that because I was poor and Hispanic she could sweep me off into a heap with other girls she had discarded. She assumed I would be reluctant to stand up for myself for fear of causing offense.

But my dream was far more important to me than pleasing her.

As I walked home, I thought how this must happen all the time to people with even less resources—and nerve—than I. Hadn't my mother's family done the same thing to her when they discouraged her from going to college?

How many people in my neighborhood had big dreams before someone kicked the ladder out from under them?

How about Sammy the junkie, who nodded off in front of the dry cleaner's every night? And Lupita, the single mother who struggled to buy formula for her twins? What had they once dreamed for themselves?

The next day I stepped into the ring for the first big fight of my life.

I marched into the Board of Education office, snagged the assistant superintendent of schools, and told her my story.

"I'm applying to these colleges," I told her. "My counselor won't send my transcripts. I want you to do it for me."

I didn't say *please, I wish, I'd appreciate,* or *would you mind?*

I didn't justify my feelings.

I didn't get into a dialogue or invite discussion.

I said what I wanted, directly and to the point.

"Okay, okay!" the woman said, holding up her hands. Maybe she smelled a court case in the air.

Next, I went to see the principal and spoke to him in the same forthright way. I saw that I didn't need to be hostile or insulting to hold my ground—just strong. "This is what I need," I told him. "This is what I want."

And it worked. He became one of my strongest allies.

He ended up overseeing my college recommendations,

and I got a much stronger endorsement than I would have ever received from the guidance counselor alone. As a result, I was not only accepted by every school I applied to, but I ended up with a scholarship to Wellesley.

I had fought and I had won.

ROUND 2

This victory was a personal milestone, a turning point on my road to empowerment.

But I couldn't climb out of the ring just yet. In fact, I was in the middle of a three-round bout; I just didn't know it.

I faced another battle at home. My parents, extended family, and several church members were horrified that I wanted to move to Massachusetts and attend Wellesley.

"What's the matter with a city college?" they asked me. "Why do you have to go so far away?"

If I had been planning to get married, I could have moved to Timbuktu and nobody would have cared.

But there was another reason my family was so discouraging. They agreed with the guidance counselor that Wellesley was no place for a girl like me.

"Massachusetts is too far! You won't know anybody. You'll never fit in."

My parents tried cajoling me, then forbidding me, but none of it worked.

"Those poor Rosados," church members said, shaking their heads. "There's no controlling that Debbie."

The night before my departure, I sat at my window, looking out at the kids playing stickball in the alley, the old women catching a breeze on the stoops, the tough boys strolling by with their menacing walk.

I was leaving a sheltered Latino world, a separate universe where everyone spoke Spanish and listened to salsa music and ate rice and beans.

Wellesley, on the other hand, was a refined, all-female, mostly white, liberal arts college with an atmosphere as different from my urban landscape as the moon.

On my visits, I'd been enchanted by the beautiful lakeside campus nestled among ancient oaks and weeping willows. I was in awe of the castlelike dorms with their huge fireplaces, where I could just see myself basking in the glow of cozy blazes while reading a book in one of those comfy, winged-back chairs. I was impressed by the tea and crumpets served on Fridays and the "socials" with Harvard boys.

After city life, entering Wellesley was like stumbling into an English novel. Plaid skirts, hushed halls, tolling bells, and ivy. It was a break from everything I'd ever known.

And I was completely unprepared for the culture shock.

I should have known trouble was brewing. Earlier in the year, my roommate-to-be, Miss Morgan Taylor Baker,* sent me a note on beautifully engraved stationery asking whether we should both bring our stereos. In the note, she also let me know of her musical preferences, and she mentioned that she'd gotten into Harvard but that her parents hadn't let her attend because it was too "liberal."

I didn't even own a stereo. I'd managed to scrape up just enough for a clock radio—and I didn't recognize any of the music she mentioned. Who the heck was Joan Baez?

---

*Not her real name.

But I was still firmly on cloud nine and didn't see the hurricane that was heading right my way.

The storm slammed into me during my first day on campus.

When I entered my dorm room with my bulky suitcase, I found the entire Baker family, an icy-looking couple in their forties with their preppy daughter.

"Hi," I said. "I'm Debbie Rosado."

I was raring to go. On my own and out of state! I could hardly contain my excitement.

But why did this couple have such odd looks on their pinched faces? Did they smell something bad?

They took one long look at me, then exited without a word, Morgan following.

When she eventually returned, I asked, "Why'd your parents rush out like that?"

At least she had the decency to blush.

"They don't want me rooming with you," she said. "Sorry, but they'd like you to move to another room."

Within an hour of my arrival, my dream had been shattered.

Humiliation.

I thought I'd known what that word meant, but it took on new meaning that day.

I'd believed that once I left my old life all my problems would vanish. Without a past, I'd create a new future. I'd become anyone I wanted to be.

But miles from my old neighborhood, I had been pegged and categorized as a ghetto kid. I wasn't sassy Debbie Rosado, just an anonymous, nonwhite face.

I was devastated, but whom could I tell?

Not my parents; I already knew what they'd say: "We told you so!"

I tried confiding to a campus counselor, telling her my story in a rush of indignation. But I could tell by her pursed lips that she didn't sympathize with me either.

"Maybe you should go back home if you find it so unpleasant here," she said when I finished.

So, at sixteen I had to stand firm and fight for my dream, which was still new and fragile, in its infancy.

I was terrified, especially when the dean, a cool matronly woman, called me into her office.

There she sat, straight and stiff, no makeup, and dressed in gray—the opposite of every warm and vibrant woman I'd ever known in my old neighborhood.

"You *are* here on a full scholarship, Deborah," she said meaningfully.

"I realize that."

"Don't you think it would be advantageous to simply cooperate with the housing bureau and move to another room?"

I might have been alone and overwhelmed. But by then I was also pissed.

"Are you saying I'll lose my scholarship if I don't agree to move?"

"No," she said. "I'm not saying that."

I was a tangle of insecurity, homesickness, and bruised feelings. But I wasn't going to let her see that.

"Does Morgan Baker have more right to be in that room than I do?"

"No, I'm not saying that either," she said coolly.

"Good," I said, standing. "Because I'm not budging."

I investigated my rights, then stood firm and watched everyone scuttle around me.

A few days later, Ms. Baker unhooked her stereo, packed her button-down oxford shirts, and moved to another room.

I won—without arm wrestling her or knocking the dean out of her overstuffed chair.

This experience helped me see how emotionally strong I could be. It made me realize that I could take a lot of heat.

This became important later in life. When I became a blacksmith, forging a company, and had to pitch my business and call on people who weren't welcoming, I was ready. I'd been in training for years.

LEARN TO BOB AND WEAVE

Business is relentless. It's fierce and competitive. If you disappeared from the universe right now, the world of commerce would keep on spinning. Phones would continue ringing, and someone would slip right into the spot you vacated.

No one is going to postpone a board meeting because your feelings are hurt or halt production because you need time to lick your wounds.

No one cares if you're having a bad hair day, a PMS attack, or a perimenopausal moment.

I know; it's humbling. Go ahead and cry if you have to, then face it and toughen up.

In case you still need convincing, here's what happened to me on one of those typical poop-hits-the-fan days; I've had a lot of those in my business life.

Early in the morning, I received a phone call from my baby-sitter saying that she couldn't pick up my five-year-old son from the bus stop because she was sick. My backup sitter also fell through, and I was swept up in a storm of activity, trying to get everything finished so I could leave the office by a quarter after two.

Phones were ringing off the hook. Everybody wanted a piece of me. I was juggling vendors, deadlines, and deals, hosing down one fire while dousing another. My head was a jumble of design specifications, phone numbers, costs per unit.

As usual, I hadn't even stopped for lunch, just tried to discreetly munch an apple as I listened to a salesman rattle on.

In the middle of all this, I received a call from my mother. Her multiple myeloma, a bone cancer, was aggressively advancing, and she was calling me to vent her pain and terror. Even at this sad point, however, she was most worried about everyone else. She was unable to put herself first, even as she faced death.

As soon as I hung up, the phone rang again, and this time it was my brother, who needed help navigating the medicare bureaucracy to get the dialysis treatments he needed to stay alive. I spent another half hour listening to him, helping where I could, all the while feeling more frantic and exhausted.

When I finally got off the phone and looked at the clock I couldn't believe it was already two-twenty! If I ran, I could just make it to the bus stop in time to pick up my son.

I grabbed my jacket, rushed out the door, and almost knocked over a man who was walking in with a clipboard.

"I'm from the Consumer Safety Testing Commission," he said, showing me his card.

"What can I do for you?" I asked without enthusiasm.

"We've been called to investigate a complaint. Someone claimed they got hurt with one of your products."

This was the first I'd heard of the problem, but I didn't have time for another headache.

"Look, I'd be happy to talk to you later, but I've got to run," I told him. "Let's make an appointment, and I'll give you whatever you need."

To my surprise, the man became confrontational. "I don't want to come back later," he told me. "I need to talk to you *now*. You can either give me the information I need or I'll have every document in this office subpoenaed by tomorrow."

I felt steam building in my head. I was so stressed out that I felt like screaming or crying—the last thing I wanted to do in front of this guy.

And in my mind's eye I could see my little boy getting off the bus in the snow, looking around, and realizing no one was there to pick him up. I remembered how it felt to be lost and forsaken. And I couldn't bear for him to experience that.

But the bully from Consumer Safety didn't care about my tender feelings; he wasn't concerned about my son, by this time standing alone and bewildered at the side of the road.

So I had to stand up to him, coolly and dispassionately.

"You wait right there while I make a call," I told him.

I phoned my attorney. "There's some guy from Consumer Safety here who's saying he'll be back with trucks to shut down my whole operation if I don't provide him with information he wants right now. Can he do that?"

"No," my attorney said very clearly. "He can't."

I hung up and went back to where I had left the man.

"Listen, my attorney just informed me that you can't make an immediate demand for this information. If you want to make an appointment with my secretary, fine. But I don't have anything more to say to you now."

I swept by him and left.

And what do you think happened?

No subpoena, no trucks, no shutdown.

He backed down, as bullies usually do. He made an appointment, we went over the paperwork, and I supplied him with all of the information he requested. (By the way, after months of investigation it was determined that we had not only complied with existing safety standards but had gone beyond all established requirements. The complaint was determined to be frivolous, and the entire case was closed.)

There are times when a bully blocks your path, and you're going to have to know how to bob and weave to get around him, under him, or even right over the top of him. No one else can do this for you. Nor would you want another person to; in the end, it's actually quite satisfying to leave the bullies behind, surprised and defeated.

PRACTICE SELF-DEFENSE

Loretta Sanchez found out how to do this for herself.

A young and fiery former businesswoman, Sanchez ran for Congress in conservative Orange County, California, against Republican Congressman Bob Dornan. No one, least of all Dornan, expected a Hispanic, a newcomer, and a Democratic female without political experience to beat him.

The vote was close, but she won.

Dornan was so shocked by Sanchez's narrow win that he insisted on a recount. Then he challenged her victory by claiming she was involved in voter fraud and that she had gotten illegal aliens and other non-U.S. citizens to vote for her.

Despite being duly elected, Sanchez had to spend her own time and money to fight the House majority party's efforts to take her congressional seat away.

Her battle with the Goliath of entrenched male politics incited women from all over the country to open their pocketbooks in support of Sanchez's right to her legitimate victory.

Congressional women across party lines stood united behind Sanchez. She became a heroine to thousands of women who said they were no longer willing to have what was theirs taken away.

Fifteen months and hundreds of thousands of dollars later, the task force that investigated Dornan's vote challenge was unable to prove his charges.

Sanchez had taken on the bully and won.

This is the same woman who sat down and sewed her own inauguration gown.

That's power.

FACE OFF IN NEW AND DIFFERENT WAYS

I'm not gonna lie to you.

When you climb into the ring, there's a pretty good chance you'll come away with a few bruises. To survive, you have to develop a muscle that allows you to react by choice and land a right hook that's about effectiveness, not ego. Part of that is using your anger to see what you're really committed to, then moving in the most powerful way possible.

My agent, Rusty Robertson, is one of the best fighters I've ever seen in action. Recently she was telling me a war story about closing one of the biggest deals of her career.

Years ago, when she was a neophyte in the public relations and marketing business, Rusty scored a presentation to a group of powerful investors for a potential multimillion-dollar project. Inexperienced, nervous, and facing some of the toughest and most influential people in network broadcasting, she laid out a complete business plan for her idea. At the end of the presentation she found herself looking up at a sea of sarcastic faces. Then, from across the table, she heard the key investor saying, "You're nothing but a huckster!" She decided to not react in the moment and possibly blow the whole deal. She chose to suppress her feelings and privately die a thousand deaths.

Insulted and angry, Rusty finished her presentation, went home, and looked up the word *huckster.* She learned that it meant "a person who sells wares in the street; a peddler, particularly that of fruit and vegetables."

She could taste closing this deal and knew she could win if only she made the right move. She remembered that the key investor really liked tomatoes, so she decided to send him a HUGE basketful. Rusty wrapped a big red ribbon around the basket and signed the card "from your friendly huckster."

Well, he really got a kick out of that. They closed that deal—and went on to many others, exceeding over $100 million dollars in business. Over time this investor and Rusty became very good friends, and he learned to respect her creativity and energy.

Sometimes the right move isn't a swift right upper cut. As Rusty says, "Sometimes the winning move is a bushel of tomatoes and a dose of chutzpah!"

DO YOUR HOMEWORK

In 1990, Dr. Antonia Coello Novello, a native of Puerto Rico, became the first woman and the first Hispanic to serve as Surgeon General of the United States. Appointed by President Bush, she found herself immediately facing the new health threats confronting the nation. This post would test a lifetime of training and require compassion, hard work, skill, and a commitment to succeed.

As Surgeon General, Dr. Novello led the nation's fights against smoking and AIDS, advocated for improved diet and nutrition, and stressed the importance of immunization and disease prevention.

Novello's childhood had been marked by a painful chronic illness of the colon, a condition that would be surgically corrected at age eighteen. Her experience led her to vow to address the suffering of others and the decision to obtain a degree in medicine.

She went on to become a professor of pediatrics at Georgetown University, a Deputy Director of the National Institutes of Child Health and Human Development, and a congressional fellow on the staff of the Labor and Human Resources Committee.

On the frontline of pediatric AIDS research and the workings of a national network for acquiring, allocating, and transporting human organs for transplantation, Novello trained long and hard to recognize when to use confrontation, when to use the element of surprise, when to take on Goliath, and when to walk away to fight another day.

Fueled by a responsibility to be a voice for those who cannot speak for themselves, Dr. Novello continues to fight on in her current post as Commissioner of Health for the State of New York, where she works to provide health care for vulnerable children in order that they may grow up strong, with the chance for the kind of education and success that she has had. One of her most cherished "war trophies" is the request from the Smithsonian to obtain her Surgeon General's uniform for display in their collection.

I once asked her, "What is your single most effective fight strategy?" She answered, "Don't pout, prepare. You can't be fueled by emotion alone. Power comes from the person standing in a position of truth and armed with the right data, the right facts, and the right information."

If you intend to win, make sure you do your homework.

PICK YOUR BATTLES WELL

If you squander your energy fighting every little skirmish, you'll be depleted when you need to fight the important battles. You'll know when it's time to raise your dukes; you'll feel it in your gut.

When another kid called my son a "Puerto Rican shit" at school one day after there was a big blitz about me in the press, I didn't have a moment's hesitation. I knew I had to fight.

But first I had to get over the sting.

The slur had hurt me as much as my son. I'd let myself be lulled into a false sense of security by moving my family to a small town in suburban New Jersey. I thought I'd found a place where I could rest and where my kids would be really safe. My kids were growing up surrounded by horse farms and antiques shops, and I was pretty sure they wouldn't be faced with the terrors that had haunted my childhood: street gangs and drug addicts, dead bodies in front of the door. But I'd forgotten that racism lives in every zip code.

I made an appointment at the school. Then I met with the principal, the parents, and the child to make sure the incident was handled seriously and wouldn't happen again.

I showed up and fought for my son so that he would know it was essential.

At the same time I initiated a dialogue with him, stressing two points: "The first thing I want you to realize is that there are some things in life you don't have to tolerate. I want you to let me know if anything like this comes up again, and we'll deal with it. But the second thing I want you to remember is even more important: what the world thinks of you doesn't matter. *It's what you think of yourself.*"

He got it. I could see it in his face.

USE THE ANGER

What would you do if you were pregnant and found out you were HIV positive?

If you're like most women in South Africa, you'd keep silent and pray.

That's what Mercy Makhalemele did—at first. She kept

her condition to herself and prayed each day that her child would be born without the dreaded virus.

In South Africa, one out of three mothers passes the virus on to her baby. These children often live and die alone, abandoned and unclaimed by relatives who don't want to be stigmatized.

Mercy managed to keep her HIV status secret until the morning she gave birth, when the nurses read it on her chart. Afraid to even touch her, they left her alone, unattended.

And then the tragedy continued: Mercy discovered that her newborn daughter was also HIV positive.

Then, as now, there were more people infected with HIV in South Africa than in any other country in the world. But the disease was rarely discussed. People with AIDS were afraid they would be cast out of their homes or lose their jobs if their condition became known.

The tragic story of one woman, Gugu Diamini, has become a cautionary tale for many South African females. In 1998, after she admitted being HIV positive, she was stoned to death by a group of young men who claimed she had shamed their community.

Mercy waited eight months before she told her husband, Sam, that she had the virus. Although Sam had given her HIV, he didn't believe he was infected. When Mercy revealed her condition, he not only beat her and threw her out of their house, but he also revealed her status to her boss.

But Mercy's troubles weren't over: Her husband died of AIDS in 1994 and her daughter in 1995, at the age of two and a half.

What would *you* do if you lost your job, your husband,

and your child to a virus—one that threatened your own life?

After these deaths, rather than surrender to inevitable defeat, Mercy became a warrior dedicated to fighting her two most formidable enemies: AIDS and the stigma that created the silence about it.

How did she find the courage?

Mercy embraced her roots. Her tribal name means "green tiger," a reference to the peace-loving nature of her ancestors. Generations of her people had endured many injustices, including her father's imprisonment during apartheid.

Gaining strength from her people's gentle manner, Mercy began to work on mobilizing and sensitizing people to the human suffering behind the silence.

By challenging the stigma associated with AIDS and reaching out to others, Mercy was able to transform her anger into a healing force, thus rejuvenating herself and enabling her to survive.

"I was so consumed by anger that the only relief was to find a way to love people, to have compassion for those who are ill," she told me.

Mercy Makhalemele has now become one of South Africa's most prominent AIDS activists, recently organizing a women's satellite AIDS conference in South Africa as part of the XIII Annual International Aids Conference.

"I can't keep quiet," she says. "My whole family was shattered. This thing has taken everything I ever wanted to have as a young woman. Now the thought of that, thinking of all the young women and men in this country, [it] just drives me nuts to think South Africa has fought so much to get where we are today. Why should we lose all these opportunities for our young African men and women because of this disease?"

KNOW WHEN TO
THROW IN THE TOWEL

If there's an art to fighting, there's also an art to letting go.

For a long time I was embroiled in a battle that was beginning to sap all of my energy. It was a big relief—and a great lesson—when I realized the war was over and the time had come to retreat.

After I left my father-in-law's enterprise to begin my own company, a family member, who had been a former co-worker, turned nasty. He started spreading rumors and making untrue accusations. He began calling accounts and advising them to not have any dealings with my husband or me. My father-in law had just had quadruple-bypass heart surgery and was unable to intervene.

Here I was, a young mother, trying to wrestle my own challenges and forge a new business, and everywhere I turned this man was blocking my progress with rumors and slander.

It was like something in a Stephen King novel; he was around every corner, a nightmare that just wouldn't go away.

At one point, I was sitting with a buyer at Caldor, a regional discount chain. I was on my way to closing a piece of business when she said, "You know, somebody just called the office this afternoon and said we shouldn't meet today because they're in litigation with you."

The accusation was untrue, but it still rattled me and sidetracked my presentation. I had to spend some of my sales time explaining the situation.

Months passed, and just when I would think the attacks had ended, they'd start up all over again. I felt as if I were swimming against the tide, defending myself against this constant slander. It was exhausting and infuriating.

Then it dawned on me that this man wasn't just hurting me; by extension he was harming my children.

This realization mobilized me to battle.

I'd wanted to handle this issue within the family, but my former colleague turned enemy forced my hand.

Gathering my forces, I began my attack. I hired lawyers, and we threatened to prosecute the entire company for his actions.

When I took this step and followed through, the personal attacks finally stopped, but the whole process took years. Yet even after it was over, I held on to the residue of the fight, keeping the fire of it alive in my body and mind.

Some nights I couldn't sleep, reliving my outrage and concocting plots of revenge. I continued to feel exhausted and bitter, even when there was no enemy left to fight.

I began to see that I was poisoning myself with this kind of thinking, tying up all the creativity and energy I needed for my own projects. So I made a deal with myself.

I decided to let go of my bitterness for a day and see what it felt like.

It was great. My whole body felt lighter, as if I'd taken off a suit of armor. People smiled at me more often, and my face didn't look pinched in the mirror.

It felt so good, in fact, that I extended it to another day, and then the next. I began meeting new people and having fresh ideas.

I began to see that my whole world was starting to move forward now that I wasn't hip-deep in resentment. Without all that poison clogging my system, my creativity could flow again.

The art of letting go is just as important as the art of fighting.

You have to know when to lay down your weapons and gather your energy for a new bout.

HOW TO HAVE GRACE IN THE RING

Don't Stew

You can't be a good fighter if you're a steaming cauldron of old wounds and slights. The more you manage your emotions, the less they'll manage you. If you have a disagreement or misunderstanding, work to get it cleared up as soon as possible.

Try this:

1. On a piece of paper, write a list of disputes that are currently taking up emotional space and roughly date when they occurred.
2. On a second sheet, make two columns. Label one "active" and one "inactive."
3. Take a look at the list of disputes. Place any dispute that you haven't actively dealt with in over a month under "inactive," then black it out using a heavy marker. Have you been feeling bad about a slight your boss or mother-in-law made six months ago, when you first got your job? Put it under "inactive" and cross it out. Are you still smarting about that competitor who stole away your client eight weeks ago? That's ancient history, too; place it under "inactive."
4. Place anything less than a month old under "active."

Now, address the active issues. You don't have to get into a catfight and throw the person into the gutter. Simply voicing your issues often takes the air out of a conflict . . . and allows you to move on.

For example, if you're steaming over the way a colleague once spoke to you, deliver a simple assertive message using the following guidelines:

- ◆ Speak directly.
- ◆ Don't undercut your position by using words like *I wish* or *please.*
- ◆ Don't phrase your statement as a question.
- ◆ Don't offer a false apology if you did nothing wrong.
- ◆ Make a specific request.
- ◆ Get a commitment.

Try something like: "I was upset by the way you publicly criticized me at yesterday's meeting. In the future I expect to have such discussions in private. Can you agree to do that?"

Most people don't get called on their behavior, and so they walk around oblivious to what damage they cause. More than likely, your colleague was unaware of your displeasure and will say, "Oh, sorry. I didn't realize. Next time I will."

Of course, she might also tell you to shove it. And then you'll need to decide whether to drop it or continue to round two. Either way, the idea is to get it off your own plate. Voicing your complaint shuts off this energy siphon and allows you to move on.

Stage a Win/Win Bout

I can be a pit bull if I have to, but who wants to live a dog's life? Before you bare your teeth, bristle your back, and jump into the fray, make sure your opponent isn't worth more alive—and in your corner—than dead. Often, your goal shouldn't be to rip someone to shreds and stand gloating over the corpse. Sometimes your goal should be to find a way to join forces, so together you can emerge victorious.

That's what Alice Borodkin did.

As the publisher of a Denver newspaper, the *Women's Business Chronicle,* for female professionals and busines women, she faced two threats. The first was the large and wealthy area newspapers, which were beginning to take notice of the lucrative professional women's market. The second threat was smaller and more personal: another woman across town who published a four-color magazine, *Zenith Woman Magazine,* which was already in direct competition for the same niche.

Although Alice and her immediate competitor, Judy, knew each other, they had little personal contact. They were civil when they met at business functions, but that was all.

Then Alice's husband died, and Judy did something that women find natural: she reached across the ropes of competition and expressed her sympathy by sending Alice a condolence card.

This act of kindness made an impression on Alice. After that, whenever she and Judy found themselves together at functions, they began to chat about their lives. And when Alice remarried, she included Judy on her invitation list.

"You know how women connect; we always connect. We

talk about our lives; we're open with each other," Alice said. "Women can't help but do it, even when we're competitors."

Soon their conversations turned to business and the threat they both faced from the giant newspapers.

At one dinner, as they stood talking together, a colleague walked by, saw them, and said, "Oh, you two together, this means trouble."

A lightbulb went off. *Trouble.* Maybe she was right.

The more they talked, the more Alice and Judy realized that they were each too small to hold their own separately in a long battle with the newspaper giants. But if they consolidated their resources instead of squandering their energy competing against each other, they might become a greater force that *could* thwart the big guys.

And that's what they did.

These two former competitors made a shrewd and powerful move: They became allies.

Their first project together, producing a yellow pages for women in the Denver area, was such a success that they decided to continue to pool their complementary skills. Together they continue to publish the newspaper, the magazine, the yellow pages, and now the *Women's Network Reference Guide.* Their circulation is now 55,000, more than triple the circulation of either of their former publications.

"It took time to trust each other," Alice said. "But now I trust Judy with my life. Instead of knocking our heads against the wall separately, now we work together. Instead of one David fighting against Goliath, now there are two."

As a result of their alliance, the two women have branched out in directions that were unforeseen to them before, offering consulting services to companies who want to understand the market. And Alice is making a bid for a state house seat.

As women, we're champs in forging personal relationships and fostering cooperation. In terms of building alliances, we have it all over men.

Take another look at someone you've perceived as a threat, someone you may have been watching from a distance. Is there a way the two of you might be able to link up and combine your talents and resources?

Have the courage to extend a hand to a worthy opponent, and your reward might be a powerful ally.

WHAT THE PROS DO

Train with the Best

There are so many battles in the world worth fighting: ending world hunger, eradicating poverty, and providing a first-class education to all, for example. Volunteer, grassroots, and advocacy groups are great training camps where novices are welcome; these groups are often understaffed and underfunded. Find a cause that really gets you charged and an organization with a well-developed fight strategy. You get a practice mat; they get you.

Celebrate the Wins

List the battles you've won, then hang the list on the wall to remind yourself of your own capacity to win. Whether you've stopped smoking or landed an account you fought hard for, make sure you savor your successes.

COMMON MISTAKES
ROOKIE FIGHTERS MAKE

Get Cocky

If you're cocky in the ring, you can cause serious dam-age. I know. In early rounds I've been fired, lost money, and ruined relationships, all because of arrogance run amok . . . mine, that is.

Take Risks You Can't Afford

If you can't afford to lose, don't climb into the ring. Fate might reward courage, but not stupidity. What will happen if you lose the bout? No matter how high your odds of win-ning, there's always a chance you'll end up on the mat, and it's a foolish person who doesn't consider that possibility and prepare for the consequences.

Don't Listen to the Corner

Of course, this assumes you have someone in your corner you can listen to. If you find yourself in a difficult position with no one cheering you on and giving you much-needed advice, re-read the section on finding a mentor. Don't wait until you need that indispensable ally to recruit one!

Don't Choose Your Opponents Carefully

If you climb into the ring with Evander Holyfield, somebody's probably gonna die—and it ain't Evander. Pick your opponents carefully, because when you're going at it toe to toe—or fist to face—you're going to pay the price for those choices. Know your own strengths and weaknesses, but know your enemy's too . . . *before* you climb over those ropes! Once you're in the ring, it might be too late.

Be Ashamed to Run!

If you're already in the ring and realize that you're outclassed, don't allow misplaced pride or stubbornness to keep you from making a graceful, speedy exit. Some forces can't be fought; they're too strong. And the only way to win in a fight against them is to surrender. There's no shame in an honorable retreat. Limping out of the ring is better than being carried out on a stretcher with a tag on your toe and a lily on your chest. At least you'll be alive for Round 2.

Fight to the Death

Don't use unnecessary force. If someone commits a minor transgression against you, you don't need to kill and bury him when inflicting a simple black eye will do. Remember, we're trying to recruit allies, not make bitter, lifelong enemies. And if you've completely murdered your opponent, you might have created a corpse that's going to keep rising from the grave to haunt you, year after year. Nobody needs that!

CRISIS OF CONFIDENCE

The greatest foe in your life is *you.*
More powerful than any external force you'll encounter

are your own demons—asking if you deserve to win, reasoning that you shouldn't reach for more, immobilizing you with the fear of failure.

What can you do to slay these ominous creatures? Here's what's worked for me:

- *Focus on the end result.* Remind yourself of the payment you will receive for your present troubles and toil.
- *Play to your strengths.* Being humble doesn't mean being down on yourself; it's knowing your strengths and weaknesses and doing the best you can with what you have.
- *Know your nonnegotiable values.* Exactly what price are you willing to pay to achieve your goals? Few things in life actually come with a price tag attached. We don't usually know the cost of something until we have already made a sizable investment in it. Be ready to say "No, that's enough" and walk away. Nothing is worth the cost of your integrity, your reputation, or your self-respect.
- *Move to produce no regrets.* Ask yourself: Ten years from now, will I look back on this course of action with pride and satisfaction? Or will I be ashamed? If I allow fear and doubt to stop me from taking this step, will I mourn the loss of what might have been?
- *Remember, there are no warm-ups in life.* Each period of your life presents unique opportunities. We like to think, *It's never too late to realize my dreams.* And although we admire the eighty-year-old great-grandmother who finally gets her college degree,

she is a rare exception. Whether you want to bear
children, begin a business, become a gold
medal–winning gymnast, get a college degree, or
backpack across Europe, there are decades in your
life when these goals are more practical than others.
If you allow those opportune times to pass by, you
might find it difficult, if not impossible, to fulfill
your objectives later. Live each day as though your
dream depends upon it. It does.

◆ *Listen to your inner voice.* Not that naggy, bitchy
voice that sounds a lot like the people who may
have criticized you over the years. Learn the sound
of your true, inner voice and obey it. (A hint: Your
true internal voice will be much softer than those
other screaming meemies in your mind. Wisdom
whispers; it has too much dignity to shout.)

◆ *See the adventure in it.* So what if you fall short of
your goal—or even fail altogether? It will make a
great story for your "memory book." When you're
ninety years old and rocking in your chair before
the fireplace, you can tell your great-grandchildren
about the crazy thing you tried. A repertoire of
good stories is the difference between being old and
senile and being delightfully eccentric.

◆ *Imagine the best possible outcome.* Okay, so the worst
might happen. But so could the best. We are always
willing to admit that something terrible might happen, something dreadful we hadn't even anticipated.
But sometimes life has pleasant surprises, too. The
results, for ourselves and for others, might be more
wonderful than we could possibly have imagined.

◆ *Find something to be grateful for.* This is the easiest, because we all have blessings all around us . . . if we only take the time to look. Make a habit of pausing and thinking of three things in your life that you cherish. Even on a PMS day when the kids have the flu, the cat got into the trash, and your business partner ran off to Morocco with his wife's poodle groomer . . . there's always chocolate.

Chapter 7

Play Beyond the Rules

"All serious daring starts from within."

—EUDORA WELTY

From the time we're zipped into pink buntings as infants, we're all in Good Girl Training. We're weaned, toilet trained, and spoon-fed a diet of obedience and compliance.

The only way to miss out on this training is to be raised on a desert island. From Don't-Make-a-Fuss to Wait-and-Be-Patient, these Good Girl messages are bred into us all.

The problem is that these messages force us to play the game with old rules that no longer apply. To dream big and live your dream now, you're going to have to learn how to play beyond the rules.

Bold women, women who are willing to push the envelope, have paved the path to dignity and power. If an unknown seamstress named Rosa Parks hadn't refused to give up her bus seat to a white passenger in Montgomery, Alabama, there might never have been a Montgomery Bus Boycott in 1955. Without people committed to the concept of personal empowerment, there might never have been the pursuant Supreme Court decision stating that Alabama's state and local laws allowing segregation were illegal.

If Susan B. Anthony and Elizabeth Cady Stanton hadn't revolted against the laws of the state—and the customs of society—who knows when women would have won the right to vote?

From Sojourner Truth to Billie Jean King to Wilma Mankiller—the first female chief of the Cherokee Nation—women who've made a fuss are the ones who've changed the world.

But those pioneers paid a price for us all; playing beyond the rules can be costly and difficult. A lifetime of conditioning can hold us back.

You might think, "This doesn't affect me. I'm a modern woman who's worked out all that stuff." But the litany of do's and don'ts is so long you might not even be aware of its censoring effect on you and your daily actions.

It's hard to break completely free from that Good Girl Training.

Just ask yourself a few questions:

- Do you need to have your decisions validated by others?
- Are you unable to graciously accept compliments?
- Do you apologize when you don't need to?
- Do you precede your statements with *I'd appreciate, I wish,* or *Would you mind?*
- Do you say maybe when you mean no?
- Do you deny yourself the things you love?

◆ Do you sidestep confrontations?
◆ Do you minimize your accomplishments?

Even if these behaviors aren't obvious issues for you, they've probably cropped up at some point in your life.

And we can all use a brushup on banishing them.

DON'T PLAY SMALL

Now that we're grown-ups—out in the world with families to manage, businesses to run, competitors to vanquish, and battles to win—playing it small isn't safe; it's a threat to our happiness, our sense of fulfillment, our very purpose for being here.

There's no reason to be bulldozed, outbid, undercut, or overlooked because we're still waiting for permission to move forward. We can't allow ourselves to get waylaid by the three P's: polite, pleasant, and passive.

By all means, retain some of what's been passed down to you. Go ahead and keep your grandmother's biscuit recipe, your Aunt Ethel's words of wisdom, and your mother's childrearing advice.

But when it comes to succeeding, consider that you'll probably be better off doing exactly the opposite of at least some of what you were taught.

BE DEFIANT!

As a kid who watched the Brady Bunch in their graffiti-free school, immaculate neighborhood, and spacious home, I grew tired of not having enough, of doing without. Staring past the steel bars my father placed on our windows to keep the drug addicts out, I'd wonder: *Will I ever really make it out of here?*

I conjured up defiant dreams that provided an escape in the middle of my mother's seizures, my brother's hospital visits, and the deafening sirens that ripped the night. And this helped me say no to the hopelessness that surrounded me.

I'm not the only one who has used this form of escape. Defiance has fueled many "unrealistic" dreams.

In 1967, when Kathrine Switzer signed up for the Boston Marathon, she did so under her initials, K. B. Switzer, because the marathon was still a males-only event. This was a time when it was still widely believed that strenuous sports compromised a woman's ability to bear children.

That's what the rules said, but Kathrine was determined to run anyway. So she tucked her hair under a cap in order to be less obvious, and began the race. Along the route, one of the officials identified her as a woman, lunged at her, and attempted to tear her number off her back as she ran. Her husband and coach blocked the man and yelled to her, "Run like hell." And that's what she did.

Despite the tension, Switzer managed to finish the race at an estimated time of just over four hours and twenty minutes. But her run created such a stir that she was disqualified and suspended by the Amateur Athletic Union.

It took five long years and an arduous battle, but in 1972 Switzer became one of nine women to legally run the Boston Marathon.

DON'T WAIT YOUR TURN— IT MIGHT NEVER COME

When I first began driving in New York City, I used to sit patiently with my directional light blinking, waiting for my turn to pull out into traffic.

I waited and waited for other drivers to let me in. I sat while the light turned, the cars sped by, and the minutes passed. And you know what? My turn never came.

It didn't take me long to realize that if I didn't nudge myself forward I could be waiting until the seasons changed.

I had to *make* it my turn. I had to nose out and create my own space.

There are other times when simply signaling your readiness isn't enough, when you have to nudge your way out there.

During my second year of college, I landed a job as a customer service clerk at a handbag and umbrella company.

I saw this job as a means to an end, a way to finance my college education, which would then propel me into my real "work," which I continued to believe would be in law. I still fantasized about becoming a female Perry Mason, standing in front of a courtroom, bringing guilty slumlords to their knees.

So I was amazed when I fell in love with the world of business. The pace, the energy, the whole cycle of making something out of nothing were revelations to me. I couldn't get enough.

For the first time in my life, I worked for the sheer pleasure of it. I gobbled up everything I could learn.

Soon I was itching to move to the next level. I went to

my boss and asked if he'd consider sending me out on a sales call. He refused for all the usual reasons.

"You're too young. You're still in school, and you're inexperienced," he said.

So I headed back to the customer service desk, and I continued answering phones and opening the mail. But it wasn't the same. I'd begun hankering for more.

One day, I received a telephone inquiry from the American Museum of Natural History. The museum requested a brochure and a salesperson to follow up.

I was supposed to report all my incoming calls to my supervisor. But I happened to know that there was no salesperson covering this account. And so the wheels between my ears started turning. All day, while I opened envelopes and fielded calls, I envisioned myself walking up to that beautiful Beaux Arts building on Seventy-ninth Street across from Central Park.

I'd loved that museum ever since I was a child gazing up at the dinosaurs and wandering through the dioramas. Growing up surrounded by steel and concrete, I was thrilled by the wonders of the natural world.

And now I became entranced with the idea that the grown-up me could go back and win the museum's account.

I decided to not wait.

It was a risky move. There was a good chance I could get fired—with or without a sale.

I was a poor student who lived from one paycheck to another. My job allowed me to eat. But I told myself that this was probably one of the few moments left in my life when I could take on risk and sort out the consequences later.

I called the museum and made an appointment. And then, without telling a soul, I got prepared. *Very* prepared. I did my research, came up with a price quote, and practiced what I was going to say.

The morning of the appointment I called in sick, put on my best dress, and boarded the train to New York.

And then there I was, heading up the staircase of that magnificent museum. To be in New York City, ascending those stairs, was a real *That Girl* moment.

I met the marketing guy, shook his hand, and followed him into his office as if I'd done it every day. I was so prepared that my presentation went even more smoothly than I had imagined. And by the time I left the office I had a commitment, just as I had planned.

But the best moment was when I walked into my boss's office with a purchase order for two thousand tote bags in my hand. The president looked over the deal . . . then at me. The expression on his face was worth all my effort. His jaw dropped, his eyes bugged, his nostrils flared; it was great!

"So, are you going to let me sell or not?" I asked him.

He did.

At nineteen I was made an account executive and given my own group of accounts to manage.

I never would have gotten where I am if I had waited patiently for my turn. And although I'm less impetuous now, I've continued to bet on what I believe. And I gamble it all—everything I am, everything I have.

Are *you* willing to take a chance—a big chance—on what you believe? Or are you waiting for someone to tell you:

- ◆ What your next move should be?
- ◆ What you're worth at the bargaining table?
- ◆ You have permission to go after that big account?

You might be sitting on the sidelines a long time.

Why not focus on what you can achieve now? Look at the resources you have and see how you can put them to use.

BE AN OPPORTUNIST

As a girl, growing up in a church parsonage, I was a regular witness to the pageant of life. Weddings, baby christenings, and funerals all took place a door away from my home. When I entered the church, I was as likely to encounter a woman lying in a casket as one walking down the aisle in a wedding dress.

Because of this I was aware of the cycle of life and death in a way that other kids weren't. I saw that this "living stuff" was serious business and that people should make the most of whatever resources they had.

Church life was what I had access to, and I used every opportunity it afforded me. I taught Sunday school; I sang in the choir; I made money playing the organ for weddings.

One day I noticed that my father's parishioners went to a bodega across the street after services to buy sandwiches and bring them back for lunch. Even as a girl I had a business sense, and this obvious loss of revenue bothered me.

"Why are we letting people go across the street to buy food?" I asked my father. "The church could use the money. Why don't we sell food to them here?"

At first, my father didn't pay attention—I was always concocting schemes of one kind or another—but then he began to see the possibilities. "Go ahead and try it," he said.

I helped organize the kitchen. Soon, each Sunday a different family was donating food, which we cooked and sold ourselves. In the months to come we generated hundreds of dollars that we used to help the poor and fix up the church.

Of course, not all my bold schemes were so successful; some of them fell flat.

When I began looking into Ivy League colleges, I seriously considered Columbia University. It cost a fortune to attend, but that didn't stop me from trying.

Whenever I ran into a wall, I looked for a way of walking around it—or knocking it down.

I put on my scheming cap. *There must be a way for me to afford getting in,* I insisted. Then a lightbulb went on. A member of my father's congregation was a sweet, devout man who worked on the cleaning crew at Columbia. From my investigations, I knew that if you worked for the university, your children could attend tuition-free. The solution was so simple I couldn't believe it. I'd just ask the man at church to adopt me! I went to the library and spent hours researching the process of adoption. I even had a meeting with the man and got his consent after making one of the first big sales pitches of my life. But I ran into a brick wall when it came to my parents.

"*No,* Debbie," they said. "We're *not* going to agree to give up parental rights."

"But ma—."

"Forget it. . . ."

That was a brick wall I couldn't knock down, so I had to accept it. But hey—I tried!

STRUT YOUR STUFF

When you eat one of Lulu's Desserts, the sweetness you taste is not just the result of the delectable ingredients Maria de Lourdes Sobrino folds into her fruit-filled, gelatin treats. It's also the sweet taste of success . . . success achieved by a woman who wasn't afraid to strut her stuff.

Sobrino believed in herself and, by insisting that others do the same, she progressed from peddling flowers in Mexico City to becoming the CEO and president of Lulu's Dessert Factory, a $10 million business in Huntington Beach, California.

As a girl growing up in Mexico, Maria loved the wiggly gelatin her mother taught her to make. Mexican gelatin—tastier and healthier than the American variety—is a common sweet, served by street vendors.

But when Maria arrived in Los Angeles in 1981 with her husband and daughter to open a branch of her Mexico City–based travel business, she was unable to locate any of these ready-to-eat desserts. The one gelatin on the market was Jell-O, and at that time, it only came in the packaged powder variety.

The next few years were difficult for Maria. She lost her travel business due to the Mexican economy, and her husband returned to Mexico. Her well-heeled relatives pressured her to come home and lead her siblings in a legal career, but she decided to remain in America.

"I believed it was a good opportunity," she said. "And I was afraid to go back to Mexico because I thought things were going to change a lot, and they did."

Then she had an inspiration: She would re-create the dessert of her childhood memories. Using her mother's recipe, Maria began her business, working alone in a cramped storefront, hand-whipping and then delivering 300 cups of gelatin each day to local stores. And she called her business Lulu's, as family and friends call her.

With no business connections and speaking little English, she found it hard to pitch her products to Americans, who didn't understand her passion for the dessert. But when Maria finally located nearby Latino communities with independent shops and bakeries that agreed to take her product on consignment, she finally found her market. The local Hispanics were as nostalgic as she had been for the treats they had eaten while strolling the plazas of their homeland.

After her success in local stores, Maria was approached by a food broker, who placed her desserts in California grocery stores. By the end of 1985, she was able to expand and move to her second production facility.

Maria hired more employees and by 1989 applied for a Small Business Administration loan in order to relocate into an even bigger facility. But this move, along with an expansion of her product line and the purchase of a new food plant and new equipment, threw her into debt and a financial tailspin.

It took her five years to climb out of the well and begin to turn a profit. But by then, her burgeoning business required an even larger, state-of-the-art facility.

Maria was on the brink of signing a construction agreement to build a new 70,000-square-foot plant when she received a call from a good friend and equipment supplier, who said, "Maria, I know you're ready to build, but before you make this decision, you need to come to L.A. and look at a food plant that's going to close . . ."

When Maria visited the Baskin-Robbins Flavors Plant, she agreed with her friend's assessment: It was ideal for her growing business.

"I couldn't believe that God sent me this gift just two days before I was to sign my contract," she said.

The only drawback was that the plant was owned by Allied Domecq, Inc., the world's second largest international spirits group. Was this global corporation going to pay attention to a forty-seven-year-old Latina immigrant?

Maria made it her business to make sure they would. The woman who had begun working alone, hand-stirring her gelatin in a storefront, was determined to make a deal with one of the leading food service companies in the world.

She pulled out all the stops to strut her stuff in a campaign that would determine her company's destiny. She sent a copy of every award, magazine article, interview, and videotape about herself that she could find to Allied Domecq. And when the company finally agreed to meet her, she told them the history of her company, how she had forged her business with only her determination and her mother's recipe on a scrap of paper.

The months of negotiations were nerve-wracking. The building was a direct purchase and Maria worried that another company with a stronger financial position would push her out.

But that didn't happen.

Maria finally received the news that she had been chosen as the buyer of this 62,000-square-foot plant. Originally producing three hundred cups of dessert a day, Lulu's now produces more than sixty million a year.

She has also become a role model and mentor for other girls and women, often speaking at schools and organizations about entrepreneurship.

After fighting hard for success, Maria de Lourdes Sobrino has gotten her just desserts, and victory tastes sweet.

ASK SHAMELESSLY

Sometimes we worry so much about being a nudge or a nuisance that we underutilize the power of asking.

At the time of my move east, Christine Todd Whitman was the governor of New Jersey. When I was in despair and on Prozac, I'd find myself looking around for women like her—trailblazers, achieving the impossible—who could inspire me to move on. One day, I started to write a letter to her, but I wasn't quite sure what to say.

I often travel around with letters in draft form, waiting for something to inspire me to finish them. One day, on a flight back from a convention, I picked up the in-flight magazine and there was Whitman's face staring out at me from a story. I decided this was a sign that I should finish the letter.

Sitting on that plane headed for Newark, the words I had wanted to say to the governor came pouring out. I wrote about a desperate time in my life when I had been without work and the state of New Jersey had come to my aid. I told her how that assistance had helped get me back on my feet, and I explained that I was now in the position to hire employees myself. I expressed my gratitude to the state. And I ended by asking Governor Whitman how I might be of service.

The timing of that letter turned out to be perfect. The governor was on the lookout for potential candidates for important board appointments. As a result of my asking, I ended up having breakfast with her and other business leaders at the governor's mansion. Ultimately, I was exactly where I hoped to be—on the New Jersey Commission on the Status of Women, where I could actively affect the lives of other women.

It's unlikely Governor Whitman ever would have sought me out for this board on her own. My appointment was a direct result of my letter, written on impulse, a seed strewn to the wind one Thursday afternoon.

MAKE A FUSS

Cecilia Pagkalinawan, the Philippine-born founder and CEO of Boutique Y3K, a leading e-commerce and e-marketing consultancy, immigrated to the United States as a girl with her family so that her brother could get medical care for his heart condition.

By the age of twenty-nine, she had become one of the hottest members of New York's Internet scene by utilizing her natural talents as a dealmaker and her willingness to make a fuss.

Curiously enough, her interest in the Internet arose from a shoplifting charge. While she was shopping with her sister in Soho one day, she forgot to pay for a pair of socks. When she tried to leave the store after paying for other merchandise, she and her sister were hauled off to a detention center in Chinatown. But the shopkeepers were messing with the wrong gal.

Pagkalinawan hired a criminal lawyer, at which point the store offered to drop the charges. But instead of making a deal, she decided to make a fuss.

She sued the store and with her portion of the settlement bought a laptop, which came loaded with Internet software. With her curiosity piqued, it was only a matter of time before she realized the enormous potential of cyberspace.

Soon she made her way to interactive agency K2 Design,

where she worked as a project director and worked her way up to vice president of the company. In 1997, she was hired as president of the e-commerce agency, Abilon Inc.

When the company lost its backing in 1998, she once again made an audacious move. Instead of quietly taking her severance package, she negotiated to forgo the money in exchange for the company itself, which she purchased for $1 and renamed Boutique Y3K.

In January 2000, Cecilia closed an investment of $15 million from Vantage Point Venture Partners for Boutique Y3K.

GENERATE GOSSIP

Make sure people are talking about you behind your back. If you're doing the right stuff, it will be good gossip that generates great opportunities for you.

Minding who you are in the presence of others isn't enough; you have to mind yourself at all times, even when you're not there. From the potential gossips' point of view, who are you, what are you committed to, and how can they count on you?

I assure you, when you show up at a meeting, everything you are and everything you do is right there with you. Your most expensive designer suit, your fancy haircut, and your Louis Vuitton briefcase are only a thin facade. Savvy people see what's below the surface: the lie you told that morning, the "sorry" you haven't said, your unpaid bills, the mess in your basement . . . all of it. Everything you say or don't say, do or don't do, is perceptible to others. They pick up everything, even if only on a subconscious level, as they continually evaluate and assess your character.

Understanding this can be invaluable. Keep your act clean, public *and* private, because you never know who's listening, watching, and observing.

A few years ago, when I started to put my thinking on paper, I wrote a series of articles for the most important trade publication in my industry, *Discount Store News.* Of course, I knew my articles would be read by influential executives in the industry—key people at Costco, Kmart, Sam's Club, Staples, Target Stores, Toys "R" Us, and Wal-Mart. What I didn't know was the domino effect I had put into play.

First came a phone call from Wal-Mart inviting me to speak at a company meeting. I accepted, and at that event I received another request to keynote for the international organization Students in Free Enterprise. This organization would later recognize me with the Free Enterprise Legend Award.

Then Wal-Mart's Minority-Owned and Women's Business Development Department invited me to explore becoming a vendor. A handful of presentations later, I had secured the first million-dollar transaction of my career. Once other retailers and corporate promotions people knew I was selling to Wal-Mart, their doors became easier to pry open.

For me, good gossip has generated new business; the privilege of speaking to over 200,000 women and business-people; countless interviews on CNN and NBC, and in *Forbes* and *USA Today;* and the day-to-day adventure of having things percolating out there.

What might you cook up with a few good deeds and a bit of the right gossip?

HOW TO PLAY
BEYOND THE RULES AND WIN

Don't Run Out of Steam

Of course, you can't be fueled only by sheer defiance. Without hard work to back it up, you'll run out of steam. I learned that after my battle with Wellesley about my dorm room. I might have won, but the fight had left me alienated and angry. So I decided to thumb my nose at the whole snotty, elitist college.

Having started my freshman year with a reputation as a troublemaker, I spiraled downward from there. I walked around campus shoeless and braless, braided my hair in cornrows, and affected a belligerent attitude. I skipped classes and didn't hand in my papers on time.

At sixteen, I partied and ignored my academics. Young and foolish, I thought I could be cute and get away with it. By the end of the year I had learned otherwise; I received a mailbox full of incompletes and an invitation to not return.

Still, I remained cocky.

So what? I said to myself. *If I have to return home, I'll just go to Barnard. That's just as good.*

But first I had to face not only my family but the whole community, including every obedient daughter from my father's congregation who had gone to community college as she'd been told.

It was humiliating to return with my tail between my legs.

There I was—rebellious, outrageous Debbie—back in

my old bedroom, on my old street . . . all the places I thought I'd escaped for good.

"So, Debbie. *Qué pasa?* Why aren't you at your fancy school?" people asked. I tried to smile and brush it off, but I was dying inside.

Then I got the knockout blow.

I'd applied to Barnard as a transfer student, certain of my acceptance. But when I opened their reply, my heart sank.

We regret to inform you . . .

They'd turned me down.

My defiance had blinded me to the fact that my Wellesley transcript had trailed after me, providing evidence of my nonproductive year.

Barnard told me to go to another college for a year, get straight A's, show that I'd matured, then reapply.

I had to mend my ways and hit the books. Defiance had saved my ego, but hard work would get me back on track.

Cut Your Losses

We all have a tough time changing.

We want things to remain the same, even when the same isn't good for us anymore. The Irish say, "Better the devil ye know than the devil ye don't." But you no longer have to languish in a job you hate or a relationship you despise. Those days are over.

Giving up on a career, an objective, or a relationship that isn't working requires courage. Accepting that a dream is dead is hard. But knowing when it's time to cut your losses and cash in your chips is a skill worth developing.

Quitting my father-in-law's business to start my own company and, later, getting a divorce were two of the toughest decisions I've ever made.

Each required a period of intense mourning before rebirth could happen. And there were many months when I dragged self-doubt and recriminations behind me like an old blanket.

Often new beginnings can't take place unless we reach closure on incomplete matters. The alternative—stagnating in dissatisfaction—would be far more debilitating. Remaining in a stressful situation can cause depression as well as a multitude of physical problems. You can literally save your own life by escaping those destructive prisons that can be as limiting as cells with actual steel bars.

Quitting is necessary. It frees up time, space, and energy that you can use to create a new world for yourself . . . a life of ample choices.

Rose A. McElrath-Slade is the president of Strategic Resources, a multimillion-dollar engineering, software, development, and management consulting business in Falls Church, Virginia.

But in 1983 Rose found herself in an abusive marriage, one that she knew had to end.

Then, on her way to work one morning, she had an experience that changed her outlook. In rush-hour traffic, a stranger rammed her car, then attacked her. Her life was saved by a passing motorist.

This terrifying incident provided the impetus for her to change her life. She cut her losses and ended her marriage; then she turned her attention toward what she really wanted, starting a business of her own.

It still wasn't easy. Less than a year later, she was diagnosed with breast cancer. But now that she was working on her own behalf, she found the strength to continue, regain her health, and build a business, which eventually booked millions of dollars in sales.

If you've tried your best, and it's still not working, better cut your losses. Putting something aside isn't an admission of failure. And just because something that was once precious and useful in your life has become no longer relevant doesn't mean it was a mistake. Like a beloved garment that once fit perfectly, felt comfortable, and kept you warm, some situations simply wear out. We change, others change, circumstances change, and it no longer serves us to remain where we are.

You don't have to say "I never should have trusted her" or "Starting that business was a stupid thing to do." You took a chance. You gambled on success. And even if that gamble didn't continue to pay off year after year, you did nothing wrong. You just need to release that which is no longer a positive, healthy influence in your life. Release it with love and thanksgiving for the blessings you reaped and the lessons you learned. Then you can move on with renewed energy.

Tell the Truth

It is important to tell the truth to each other. When I profiled one businesswoman's audacious methods for securing success, she wrote me a note saying she didn't want me to use her story in this book. She was reluctant to be characterized as disobedient . . . or a "bad girl." She contended that as a role model for children such a portrayal would be harmful.

Even for grown women, the bad girl label retains its sting.

But the real danger is when we conceal our true struggles and hard-won lessons from one another. When we lie to each other, we perpetuate the myths that hold us back.

To live powerful lives, we need to share our strategies and be honest about our methods, whatever they are.

Be Your Own Cheerleader

Words are very powerful, but you can't afford to wait around for other people's praise or affirmations. They might never come.

Talk to yourself like you mean business. You might feel like an idiot, walking around the house saying, "I have the power to reach my goals" or "I deserve to be successful." But you probably do the *opposite* all the time. Think of how many times you've put yourself down just today by saying, if only to yourself, "I'm fat. That was stupid. I can't handle this. I'll never make it. I want too much."

For some of us destructive self-criticism is so relentless and devastating that we literally become our own worst critics and enemies. This process can cripple you as surely as a broken arm or leg.

Your thoughts have a direct influence on your physical body. If you don't believe it, start thinking about sucking on a slice of cold, freshly cut lemon. Sour, juicy . . . squirting inside your mouth, making you pucker and shiver.

After a couple of seconds, you'll start to salivate. You might be salivating right now, just from reading this.

Thoughts translate into physical reactions. If you go around thinking *I'm sick, I'm weak, I'm old and tired,* you're not going to win many marathons.

Stop shooting yourself in the foot. Even if it seems corny, try whispering a few wonderful thoughts to yourself every day: "I'm great. I'm strong. I'm interesting." Combined with powerful action, your words can become a self-fulfilling prophecy.

Practice Assertiveness

Sticking up for yourself is a matter of practice. The more you do it, the easier it becomes.

Even an act as seemingly mundane as sending back a meal or returning a dress can help banish the overly compliant strain running through so many of us.

Don't swallow the words you want to say.

Don't overlook the undercooked fish or stuff the blouse that's too big into the bottom of your drawer.

Each week, make it a practice to commit at least one assertive action that you might normally avoid.

For example, if someone shoves in front of you in a bank line, don't bubble over with silent, internal rage.

Take a deep breath and make yourself say: "Excuse me, I was here first."

Not only will this simple statement probably be effective, it will make you feel better.

Remember: Being confrontation-phobic can be just as hard on you as being overly combative.

Get accustomed to sticking up for yourself as if you were your own best friend.

NINE MOVES TO COUNTERACT "GOOD GIRL" TENDENCIES

1. Devise an outrageous plan to get around a wall, real or imaginary, that's blocking your progress.
2. Take a look at how you're representing yourself to the outside world. If you're downplaying your accomplishments, ask a trusted and competent friend for some straight talk.
3. Change or end any relationship in which you are criticized or put down.
4. Formulate a request you could make today to get something you've been pining for.
5. List two activities you're involved in that aren't working anymore. Set a date when you can cut your losses and put an end to them.
6. Find two situations in which you can play out of bounds and still be safe, remembering that illegal or immoral actions create far more problems than they solve.
7. Write a one-page biography highlighting your achievements. Where does it look thin, and how will you fill it out?
8. Fine yourself twenty dollars every time you:
   - Say maybe when you mean no
   - Apologize for your feelings
   - Refuse to accept a compliment
9. List the ten best things about you in large bold type on a huge piece of paper. Hang the list on the bathroom wall, and make copies of it to put over the

sink in the kitchen and on your car visor. When you're stopped at a red light, flip down the visor and read your list. There's a lot of joy in finding out that you're even more wonderful than you thought you were!

Chapter 8

Build a Winning Portfolio

*"Discipline is a powerful tool
for getting what you want out of life."*

—MARSHA SINETAR

When I speak of your "portfolio" here, I'm not talking about tech stocks or index funds or tax-free municipal bonds.

I'm talking about building a treasure trove of choices—the 24-karat assets that produce what really matters: joy, power, trust, freedom . . . wealth.

This is a who-you-are, not a what-you-own, portfolio.

Whether you're a seasoned pro or just getting your feet wet, you have to use a disciplined, systematic approach. And yes, there are many ways to go about this. But unless you've got a surefire plan for winning the lottery, you need to learn some strategies for self-investment.

START EARLY

If I can go from no money and no contacts to a life of great joy and satisfaction, and a vast menu of choices, just about anyone can.

It's a question of investing in yourself. And the sooner you start, the greater your assets will be.

My early ambitions weren't about building wealth or accumulating power. I didn't even know what they were.

I thought wealth meant having an extra fifty dollars in your pocket; I thought power was something the electric company switched off when you didn't pay your bill. As I started to move about the world, I quickly learned that accumulating power is about building a winning portfolio of assets and that my most essential investment was going to be my education.

In the summers, when I was growing up, our church was a federal free lunch distribution center. By the time the doors opened at eleven in the morning, there was always a long line of hungry children anxious for a lunch of rubbery bologna on tough-as-cardboard buns. One of my chores was to confront the sea of young and hungry faces when we ran out of food. The look on their faces as I turned them away has always stayed with me.

We were poor ourselves, but we didn't have to depend on free lunches. Yet I knew that if I didn't do everything in my power to study and get an education, I might end up in similar straits.

Because of this, education has always been critical to me, a matter of survival. I have a tremendous appetite for learning and make sure I'm well fed every day. I've made huge investments in myself by taking courses, attending seminars, and reading whatever I can get my hands on.

When I'm reading a book or learning a new skill, I feel that I'm making vital deposits into the account of my life. I'm affirming that I'm worth it, that I'm a good investment.

DIVERSIFY YOUR HOLDINGS

I would soon realize that, even if I became really knowledgeable, it wouldn't be enough. I needed to broaden my position by building a powerful network of relationships.

In America, we like to believe that success occurs because of individual effort. Most of the stories we hear are about the solitary hero or heroine, fighting without help—or even encouragement—from the cold, cruel world. But, in truth, few individuals achieve their victories without assistance. Most successes result from group efforts.

If we are unaware of those working behind the scenes, it's because networks are mostly invisible. When we observe Rosie O'Donnell, Katie Couric, or Barbara Walters, we're blind to the intricate connections that surround and support them.

But behind every successful woman there radiates a complex web of affiliations, a strand of networks that has been woven and maintained over time.

When you're down on your luck, when you lose your job or your confidence, you're not going to rush to the bank and embrace your 401(k)s. You're going to reach out to the people you know and trust.

I think of my personal network as one of my most precious assets, a gorgeous necklace that grows more valuable with time, like the add-a-pearl-necklaces the girls in my neighborhood received for Holy Communion. Each new contact is another pearl on a strand I hope to continue adding to for the rest of my life.

Build your relationship assets. Cultivate trust. Forge powerful allies. In good and bad times these people will make all the difference.

BUILD A SAFETY NET

Networking provides a solid foundation for you and the world you're creating. And no matter who you are, you can't do without it.

Heidi G. Miller, voted by *Fortune* magazine as the second most powerful businesswoman in the country, felt so lonely as a female in senior management that she organized Women and Co. This conference of top women executives, which included Martha Stewart, met in Palm Beach, Florida.

"Men play golf and do business," Ms. Miller said. "Well, we had facials and talked finance!"

As women, networking comes naturally to us. We're generally the ones who weave the complex, connective threads of daily life.

Men might hold back from asking directions, but we're quite comfortable hanging out the window, sharing advice and know-how on everything from how to set up a web site to finding a baby-sitter.

Networking is a potent method for developing relationships, fostering new contacts, and nurturing old ones. It's also a great way to increase your visibility and add to your range of information.

What can you expect from networking? A lot, according to the *Wall Street Journal,* which reported that over 90 percent of job seekers claimed that networking made an enormous difference in their successful career searches.

Through networking you can jump to the head of the line to get help with projects or receive career advice. You can get an inside peek into what it's really like to work in a field or an organization. It's also a way of gaining valuable insight on the training and aptitude necessary to break into a new field.

Networking comes in all kinds of guises . . . having dinner with an old college friend to see how she likes owning her own business, schmoozing at a party with a new acquaintance who has the job you've always wanted, or meeting with a former co-worker to discuss what's happening in your field.

Don't be reluctant to contact others out of fear that you're asking too much. Most people are happy to offer a hand.

Just remember that the "net" won't "work" unless you're contributing, too. If you're going to reel in a good catch you can't do it without sharing the bait.

PROTECT AGAINST RISK

At the lowest points in my life, networking has been a lifeline. When I've been without money and stuck, I've been saved by the power of people.

I first realized the force of networking after I was asked

to move out of my dorm room at Wellesley. I knew there was no way I was leaving, but I wasn't sure how I was going to fight.

Was I going to have to stand in the line of fire by myself?

Was I going to have to confront this prestigious institution on my own?

For days I dragged around, feeling ostracized and wounded. Overnight, my collegiate dream had vaporized into thin air.

I'd never felt like such an outsider. What was I doing going to a college where I was surrounded by the daughters of ambassadors and South American presidents? Why was I trying to fit in with this perfumed elite, glinting with gold jewelry, their noses in the air?

So it was a relief when I discovered another Puerto Rican girl from New York City. Not only had she scored almost perfectly on her SATs, she'd also managed to get straight A's at the prep school she'd attended on a scholarship.

She'd come from even more dire straits than I had—a two-room apartment in Hell's Kitchen. Everyone in her family shared the same bedroom, and she was forced to lie awake at night listening to the intimacies of her parents behind the sheet they'd made into a curtain.

One day I was in her room as she was unpacking an old radio that she'd brought in a plastic bag from New York.

As she removed it from the bag, hundreds of cockroaches scuttled out of the back of the radio onto the floor around us. "Oh, shit!" she screamed.

I was horrified for her—and myself.

I despised cockroaches; of all the things I wanted to escape, those bugs were at the top of the list. Yet even at school, four hundred miles away from home, they seemed to have followed me.

My friend and I were already considered outcasts by our snooty classmates. All we needed to cement our reputation was for a horde of roaches to swarm out of her room.

"Come on, help me!" my friend cried.

I grabbed a book and joined with her on a murderous rampage.

But I was venting more than my hatred of cockroaches. I was releasing all my anger and frustration.

After the great cockroach massacre, my friend and I did some research, and we discovered a free legal service from BLSA, the black law students' association at nearby Harvard.

The day I walked into that room of student lawyers I experienced a sense of camaraderie I hadn't felt since I'd left home.

Here were students who knew how it felt to be on the outside looking in, who'd experienced the same gut-wrenching rejection because of someone else's idea of who they were.

This solidarity was something I had taken for granted back in the city. Far from home, I began to appreciate one of the good things I'd had in spite of the poverty—the sense of community that united our neighborhood.

It wasn't that I wanted to go back to that world, but I vowed to find a way to re-create that feeling of connection in my future.

After I told my story to the student attorneys, they provided me the ammunition I needed to put a stake in the ground and hold my position.

"They can't force you out of your room," they told me.

"Yeah, but what if they take away my scholarship?"

"If they try, come back, and we'll help you. Stick to your guns."

These student lawyers didn't ask for money.

They didn't expect anything in return for their advice.

They simply extended themselves by joining my struggle, by making my problems and concerns their own.

When I walked out that day, I felt them behind me, a solid wall of support. Knowing they were there gave me strength in the days that followed, when I was snubbed in the hallways and presented with a cool wall of cashmere-clad backs.

This affiliation was a source of strength for me and reduced the risk I was exposed to in those early days.

MAKE EVERY CENT COUNT

When I first got home from Wellesley, I was looking for a job, any job. Overnight, I'd become a seventeen-year-old college dropout without support, money, or any marketable skills. At the time, of course, I didn't know the difference between one minimum wage job and another. But soon I would learn how to make every cent count.

From the pinnacle of a full scholarship at one of the most prestigious colleges in the world, I was tumbling downhill. Instead of living my fantasies of a heady intellectual life, I found myself standing in a welfare office, applying for a low-income apartment.

It was a swift and painful decline, and I was hurting. To make things even worse, I had to find a job.

The problem was that I didn't know how to do anything besides read and eat.

I was hired for my first real job, payroll clerk at New York University, only because the boss was drunk at the time of our interview. If he had been sober, I'm sure he would have noticed how miserably ill-qualified I was.

It was my duty to type out the occasional hand-processed payroll checks, and I was terrible at it. I just couldn't get all of those little numbers to fit in that tiny "amount paid" box. And I wasn't allowed to use correction fluid.

Every week, I made a pilgrimage to my supervisor's desk with a pile of botched checks until I was finally put out of my misery and fired.

And then it was back to the social services office, where they eventually helped me find a desk job in the Lyndhurst, New Jersey, Parks Department.

I tried to keep my eye on the prize of my eventual future. Barnard sparkled in the distance, the glittering goal at the top of the hill. Like the heroines in the adventure stories I'd read as a girl, I would have to trek across a broad, dreary terrain before I could get back what I had lost—my chance for a first-rate college education.

Each day, I trudged ahead. When I wasn't in class in city college or sitting somewhere with my head in a textbook, I was slumped over my desk at the Lyndhurst Parks Department, moving around dusty papers and answering the phone. It was a life of cheese sandwiches, secondhand books, circles under my eyes, and scrounging around for loose change.

One particularly boring afternoon, the supervisor of the department of public works walked over to our office.

"We need some help in our department for a few days. Is anybody interested in transferring?"

I sat up in my chair. The public works department seemed much more interesting than the parks department. For one thing, it was populated by muscular young men about whom I'd spent several weeks daydreaming as they worked outside my window in the sun.

After three seconds of contemplation, I raised my hand.

"I am!" I said.

But a month later I sat slouched over another desk, waiting for the hours to pass before I could go home. The young men and their muscles had moved on to other jobs, and the papers in public works were just as dusty, the phone calls just as mundane.

One day, a stately woman walked into the office and introduced herself as the newly elected commissioner of the department. Everyone else in our office looked exhausted and disgruntled. But this woman, in her snappy suit and suede pumps, seemed excited and alive.

"I need someone to organize my files and paperwork. Would you be interested in helping me?" she asked me.

This time, I didn't even need three seconds to make up my mind.

I was studying political science at Hunter, a city college, but nothing I was learning had any relevance to the life I was leading as a low-level clerical drone.

This new assignment would give me a chance to jump out of the dusty and theoretical into the real world. Even in a small place like the public works department in Lyndhurst, New Jersey, there were elections to be won, people to manage, and funds to fight for.

Finally I was going to get involved in some "real stuff."

The commissioner extended her hand, and I took it. I had no idea how many connections this woman had with the outside world or how much my future life would be affected by my association with her.

I only knew that I was yearning to expand myself, and she was willing to give me a chance.

Everything that came over the commissioner's desk had to pass through me first, and I absorbed it all—applying for state grants, getting budget items funded, reviewing bids for construction projects, allocating scarce resources, and keeping the electorate happy.

Under her tutelage, I learned about coalition building and the difference a great boss makes. I also learned that every dollar earned isn't equal. The $4.89 I earned each hour working for her was more valuable than the $4.89 I might have earned elsewhere.

Why? Because I received, as well as a paycheck, a role model, a great teacher, and the opportunity to discover my strengths.

Your take-home pay is not what you earn. It's what you earn plus what you learn. From that experience to the present, I've never worked anywhere or with anyone unless the "learn" outweighed the "earn." Even today, when choosing to take on a new project or embark on a new plan, a major deciding factor is how I answer this question: How much opportunity will I have to stretch and to build my portfolio?

INVEST REGULARLY

Investing includes giving to yourself *and* others—especially when you think you don't have anything to spare. You never know where the biggest returns will come from.

While I was working at the Lyndhurst Parks Department, I lived in a tenement apartment in Passaic, New Jersey. It was a dismal place with dark hallways and mice in the walls. But the worst part was the lack of heat.

In the middle of January, the radiators went cold and the pipes ran with freezing water.

The building was full of elderly poor people who shuffled out into the hall wrapped in blankets whenever this happened.

"What's wrong? Why isn't there any heat?" they always asked, as if it were the first time.

There wasn't any heat because the owner of the building, a city official, was a slumlord. He knew the old people wouldn't make a fuss.

But he didn't know about me.

I might not have had any organizing experience, but I was my parents' daughter.

I had the memory of my mother, bent over a pot in the church kitchen, hacking apart chicken wings to make a stew for hungry drug addicts. I had the image of my father, banding together with other ministers to protest police brutality in our neighborhood.

I'd spent my childhood watching my parents fight an uphill battle against poverty and injustice. They might not have had the resources to change the whole world, but they had tried to improve their little corner of it. Because of them, the stomachs of Maria Rodriguez and her four kids were full. Because of my father's intervention, Sammy Chavez and Billy Porter made it into a rehab clinic instead of ending their lives on the street.

So when I looked out into the hall at the old folks in

their shawls and blankets, the Rosado influence rose in me. Without realizing what I was doing, I began following my parents' example.

I tacked up a notice inviting people to a meeting in my apartment for the purpose of forming a tenants' organization.

I didn't expect much of a response, but when I got home from work the hallway outside my apartment was filled with excited people: old women with canes, and widowers on walkers.

The response was so tremendous that I could barely fit everyone into my freezing rooms. But that was one evening when the lack of heat didn't matter. We were warmed by our enthusiasm.

My neighbors couldn't wait to join a rent strike to force the landlord to provide the services they were paying for with their measly Social Security checks.

Standing there, watching them sign their names and donate their scrimped-for dollars, was a moment of great inspiration for me.

Because of our group's efforts, we were able to get a pro-bono attorney through the New Jersey Tenants Organization. And as it turned out, this attorney's wife was the vice president of the umbrella and totebag company where I eventually got my first big job in marketing.

So my connection to business sprang out of my organizing that tenants' meeting one bitterly cold night in my Passaic apartment. But I didn't know that then.

The thing about networking is that you usually aren't aware that you're weaving a web while you're actually doing it. You see the intricate pattern only in retrospect.

What matters is that you keep moving forward, reaching out, spinning the connections.

REVIEW YOUR PORTFOLIO

Building a winning portfolio of opportunities is an ongoing process, a habit to cultivate throughout your life.

You can't plan your retirement with a single investment made in your twenties. Your holdings need to be renewed, diversified, and updated, just as your people contacts do.

I don't want the day to arrive when I've got no game to play, nobody to call, no mischief to create. So I'm always asking myself:

What opportunities do I have? Are they enough?
What skills need improvement? Where can I learn them?
What players do I need on my team? How do I gain access to them?

Part of building your portfolio is to network strategically, locate the players you need, and put yourself in their turf. Once you get there, don't sit on the sidelines. Get on the court and make something happen.

EXPECT A WINDFALL

While you're out there making things happen, remember that everything isn't under your control. But as I found out one cold night in Washington, D.C., if you stay open to the twists and turns of the universe, an unexpected gain might be waiting for you right around the next corner.

All by myself in a room at the Willard Hotel, I could just see the White House from the corner of my window. Outside stood the frozen Capitol, but I was all keyed up inside with equal parts excitement and fright.

I had accepted an invitation to attend a National Puerto Rican Coalition fund-raiser because a friend and mentor had suggested I needed to be there.

It was possible that I might sit by myself all night, off in a corner, like a potted plant. But I had been working on being a voice for economic opportunities for women, and this coalition function was a good place to make critical contacts. Besides, Marc Anthony was the entertainment that evening, and I lo-o-ove Marc Anthony. Worst-case scenario: I'd get to hear one of the best crooners of our time, live and up close.

Lots of hair spray and a cab drive later, I was standing at the entrance to the banquet hall, handing in my invitation at the door.

Now I had to do something.

I couldn't head to the ladies' room and cool my heels in a stall until it was time to sit down for dinner. I had to propel myself out there and work that room.

I searched for someone who looked friendly *and* interesting. On my right stood a middle-aged woman who looked a little out of place herself.

"Hi, I'm Deb Rosado Shaw. What brings you here?"

"I was just asking myself that," she said. "My son's got measles, and I'm feeling guilty about not being home."

Ah, another mother.

"I know what you mean. I've got three at home."

"Three!" She laughed. "You *do* know what I mean."

And the tension blew right out the window.

This woman was also an entrepreneur, and we established an immediate rapport. In ten minutes I learned that she owned a public relations firm, was a Yale alumna, and lived half an hour away from me in New Jersey. I took her number for a friend of mine who needed help launching a new product line, and she took my e-mail address so she could send me the name of a book I was interested in reading. Others joined in, and we continued to chat until it was time to sit down for dinner.

As I was heading toward a table, I heard someone call out "Deborah!" I turned around to find a colleague I hadn't seen in over a dozen years.

"What are you doing here!" I asked, giving him a hug.

"I work for the National Institutes of Health now. Come sit at my table."

I followed him to a table that turned out to be a buffet of fabulous people.

Over the course of the meal, my friend introduced me to the former surgeon general of the United States, Dr. Antonia Novello; the station relations manager at NBCA, Anna Carbonell; and the head of the Women's Bureau at the U.S. Labor Department, Ida Castro.

Almost effortlessly, the linkages began occurring. There was a woman whose daughter wanted to attend Barnard College, so I gave her the number of a friend in the admissions office. A man on my left was a vendor to some of my retail customers and gave me the name of someone who could help me with a challenge we had.

By the time I got back to my hotel that night with sore feet and a purseful of business cards, I had reconnected with an old friend and met some wonderful new people.

Once back home, I sent follow-up notes and press kits where appropriate.

A few months later, NBCA called to see if I would do

a public service announcement during Women's History Month.

That spot played often over the course of the month and sparked new interviews with CNN, radio stations, and magazines.

You can't completely plan or predict these kinds of outcomes. But you *can* put yourself in the right place. You *can* be open and receptive. You *can* accept the serendipity of the universe's conspiring to help you.

But you *can't* sit on the couch with your feet up and wait for a windfall to come to you.

FIND GREAT VALUES

Look beyond what's obviously there.

After putting in a forty-hour week, my aunt would bring home piles of fabric scraps and sew into the night. When I visited, I loved to sit and finger these patches; the velvets and satins were the ones I loved best. My aunt and grandmother sewed and gossiped all through the evening hours, piecing together stories they'd heard during the day as they pieced together the fabric.

They knew how to "make do" with what they had. I could go upstairs to take a bath, and by the time I came back down again the remnants would have been transformed into a dress.

From them I learned about stitching together seemingly unlikely alliances and gathering together components that might not have been obviously compatible. This awareness and way of thinking about and looking at things has helped me gain invaluable knowledge.

Listen to unlikely people and look in uncommon places. I've learned plenty from standing on a coffee line or asking members of a housekeeping staff what they think of their employer.

Once I was trying to decide whether to extend credit to a huge retailer that was on shaky ground. My accounting staff did its usual thorough review, and our credit analysis bureau recommended proceeding with caution. This was a long-time customer, and I was unsure what to do.

On my next visit to the retailer, I was in the ladies' room when a few young women were standing around applying nail polish. First sign of trouble. I asked if I could borrow some polish to stop a run in my stocking. And as I freshened my makeup and fussed with my hose, I overheard information that led me to walk away from that business.

Three months later this retailer filed for bankruptcy. Had we proceeded, we might have lost over half a million dollars.

To network effectively, extend your sweep to be as broad as you can make it. And expect to find great value from unlikely sources.

SCHMOOZING 101

There's nothing new under the sun when it comes to networking and meeting people.

The old-fashioned advice for winning friends and influencing people that worked for our fathers and uncles holds true today.

Before heading out, decide:

What is my goal?
Who must I get to know to achieve it?
Where will I find this person?
What value will I bring to the relationship?

Even the most informal networking—at parties and other social occasions, for example—requires some basic preparation.

If you're attending a function:

- ◆ Arrive early.
- ◆ Familiarize yourself with the room's layout.
- ◆ Get the attendance roster.
- ◆ List the people you intend to meet.
- ◆ Work the room by having many brief conversations.
- ◆ Follow up, follow up, follow up.
- ◆ Nurture the contact.

And don't expect anyone to roll out the red carpet. If you're the new kid on the block, expect to pay your dues and prove your value.

HOW TO ADD VALUE AND REDUCE RISK

Live Beneath Your Means

You know exactly what I'm talking about here. Don't let what you really care about be held hostage by your lifestyle. I've paid for the freedom I have today by always spending less than I can afford—because building wealth is not about what you spend; it's about what you keep.

Think seriously about your own lifestyle. Are you overextended? Are you saving and investing in tomorrow? Or are you still trying to scrounge up last month's payments? Mainstream philosophy says, "You can have it all! Today!" But freedom is found in discipline. Figure out practical ways to spend less . . . even when you can afford more.

Connect the Dots

No matter who you are or what your situation, link up. From parenting to career- and business-building, there's very likely some kind of local networking or support group that's designed for your particular needs. The *Women's Venture Fund* will lend you as little as $400 to start a business; the *Women's Alliance* helps low-income women get professional attire and career skills training; and the *Committee of 200* is an invitation-only organization of preeminent business-women promoting corporate leadership.

Get on-line and start investigating local web sites or look on the bulletin boards at your local library or community center. If you can't find a group that suits you, consider starting one yourself.

Some groups I've found helpful are the National Association of Women Business Owners (NAWBO), the Women Presidents Organization (WPO), the U.S. Hispanic Chamber of Commerce (USHCC), and the Business Women's Network (BMW). But each person's needs are unique. What are yours?

Invest Responsibly

Do your research—and by all means, don't be "nice." Make sure you are taking the right course, reading the right books, networking with the right folks. If you're networking for business purposes and the group or organization you're in isn't disciplined or meanders into socializing, get out.

This is not the Miss Congeniality contest. This is about living your dream. Be conscientious when deciding where to invest yourself.

Squirrel Away

Stash those persistent messages, those thoughts and ideas that come at unexpected moments of quiet creativity. These jewels of the unconscious are valuable, yet many of us toss them away. Keep a notebook in your purse and by your bed so you can note your ideas. I've had some of my best ideas just as I'm floating off to sleep; that's when you are nearest to your subconscious and least on guard. Don't judge these thoughts, just write them down. They won't keep till morning. By the time you wake, they'll be gone.

Build Trust

In an unpredictable and turbulent world, if you can be a person whose word can be counted on, you increase your value megafold.

A while back, a senior merchandising executive at Sam's Club who had championed my company invited me into his office for a chat. Together, we reviewed the items and pricing my firm was offering to Sam's. He gave me some coaching and shared with me a valuable lesson I have never forgotten.

He said, "Deborah, underpromise and overdeliver." And although he was talking about merchandise, I have extended that idea throughout my life.

I am rigorous about the promises I make. I practice biting my tongue to avoid carelessly spewing commitments . . . a practice that is, sadly, commonplace: *Let's have lunch. I'll call you next week. Of course, I'll help.*

You can't buy trust. Trust gets built over time and must be continually renewed. Guard it with your life.

Take on Some Debt

If you're going to bring your dream to life, you *will* take on debt. I owe so much to other people, particularly to those who believed in me when I barely believed in myself, that some of these debts will never be settled.

Remember that when you ask others for help, or when they extend it of their own accord and you accept, you empower them to give. They can't make a contribution if you don't ask or you don't accept.

Generate IOUs

Honor the people who have invested in you and the gifts you've been given by passing them on to others. Generate your own IOUs, but not for the sake of getting something back. Do it so that someone else will now be in a position to pass on your gifts.

TWO TOP-YIELDING PICKS

Create an Unfair Advantage

This can be as valuable as being on that list of friends and family who got to buy into AOL.com at the insider's price. In my case, the advantage I have is that I'm a woman in a testosterone-driven industry. In a different arena, I'd be less of a novelty and would have to work differently at getting noticed.

I was recently asked how I *cope* with being in the minority. I said, "I don't. They have to cope with me. When I show up in their space, making requests, presenting offers, they're the ones who have something new happen to them. I'm completely comfortable being the only woman at a meeting, or on a dais, or at an industry event."

The advantage comes from understanding that doing what I do in a skirt often means having to be better and play more creatively. Getting pissed off isn't effective. The key is to make a high level of excellence your standard operating procedure—not because you have to but because, in the long run, it serves your cause.

Fertilize Your Brain

The reason I can hold my own with some of the most respected business leaders in the world is that I make it my business to read, and read, and read. I couldn't learn everything two days before a meeting. You can't take vitamins for a week and be healthy. Learning is a lifetime thing.

This doesn't mean heading back to school. These days, you can take courses on the Internet or learn a skill through a CD-ROM. There are weekend training seminars, personal coaches, and certificate training programs that might suit specific goals.

Fertilizing your brain keeps you young and vital. So stay on the lookout for ways to expand yourself and broaden your scope. Substitute the mindful for the mindless. Next time you find yourself sitting, eyes glazed, in front of the TV, switch it off and crack open a book instead.

THE BIG PICTURE

Time is your only nonrenewable asset. You have some now, but you don't know how much more you can count on. And once you spend it, it's gone.

Don't let others or yourself disrespect this precious gift. Every time you say *mañana* and put something off, you get shortchanged.

Recently my neighbor Karen* went to pick up her son at a basketball game and took her daughter along. Her friend asked, "Can you pick up Jake, too?

With three children who play sports, perform in bands, and are involved in all sorts of activities, I've made this request a hundred times myself. But this time was different.

On the way back home with her two children and her friend's son, a deer ran into the road. Karen lost control of her vehicle and crashed into a tree. She and her friend's son were killed.

Life is unpredictable, but we can choose how to live it. This tragedy, so close to home, has moved me to milk the ordinary moments, to be really present in every experience, every encounter.

The guy who just pumped your gas might be the last human you ever speak to. Or you might be his last. You never know. . . .

*Not their real names.

PORTFOLIO CRISIS ALERT

Investing requires making regular assessments of where you stand. Guard the health of your portfolio zealously. Be constantly alert for signs that trouble might be brewing or that stagnation might be setting in.

If, in the course of your periodic self-examinations, you experience any of the following symptoms, take immediate corrective steps.

- Your calls aren't promptly returned.
- You can't remember the last time someone asked you to serve on a board or volunteer your time.
- You don't get invited to important industry functions.
- No headhunters have called lately.
- You haven't taken a class or course or seminar in the last twelve months.
- You're in an emergency and have no one to call who can help.
- You haven't added any new contacts to your Rolodex in the last ninety days.
- You don't have three people to call right now who would give you a stellar recommendation.
- You've read less than three skill-building books in the last twelve months.
- Nobody owes you a favor.

Chapter 9

Take the Plunge

*"And the day came when the risk to remain tight in a bud
was more painful than the risk it took to blossom."*

— ANAÏS NIN

Diving into unknown waters. Challenging ourselves. Taking risks. Reinventing who we are. Who has the time—let alone the inclination—for this kind of stuff? Isn't challenge for Amelia Earhart types or for unencumbered eighteen-year-olds with time on their hands?

I hate to be the one to break the news.

It's also for *you.*

No matter what decisions you face—when (or whether) to have children, what job to take, which medical treatment to have, whether to change careers or sell your enterprise—you can't afford to be running on autopilot.

Actively designing your own path requires self-reliance, flexibility, stamina, *and* risk taking. And although this might sound intimidating, it's also a gift from life.

Choice is a privilege that often sits patiently waiting to be exercised. But sometimes we're pushed into making a decision by events over which we have no control.

Mary Bono never might have become a congressperson if Sonny Bono hadn't died in a skiing accident. Carolyn McCarthy might not have entered politics or become an antigun crusader if she hadn't lost her husband in a commuter train shooting.

Knowing which risks to take and when to take them can only come from you. The challenge is to stretch yourself *voluntarily,* before you're forced to.

DO THE NATURAL THING

A woman's very nature requires her to be fluid and able to manage change. Women are always in the process of self-creation. Transformed by pregnancy and the cycle of our womanness, we shape-shift from caregivers to bosses to mothers in the blink of an eye.

The challenge is to use this fluidity to our own benefit, to remain resilient so we can take advantage of a world brimming with opportunities.

Look around and you'll see women taking the plunge in all kinds of innovative, trailblazing directions. Hobbies are morphing into careers; pastimes are turning into paying jobs. Lab technicians are becoming psychologists and travel agents are turning into dot.com entrepreneurs as people waltz from one occupation to another.

With longer spans and broader canvases, our lives can now encompass a variety of acts . . . *if* we so choose.

Ask yourself when was the last time you really put yourself on the line or climbed out on a limb that you weren't sure could support you? When did your heart thump from something other than working out at the gym?

For some of us, it's been ages. We've nestled into our routines and rarely break a sweat.

What's wrong with that? Nothing. As long as you know this: If you're not making the choices, the choices are being made for you.

TEST THE WATERS

"Taking the plunge" doesn't necessarily mean jumping headfirst into the deep end without even checking to see if there's water in the pool. Quite the contrary. As you would do when dipping your toes into bathwater, test and test again until it feels right to immerse yourself completely.

When Massachusetts Institute of Technology (MIT) Professor Nancy Hopkins suspected she was being systematically discriminated against, she carefully tested her assumption. With a Ph.D. in biology from Harvard, Dr. Hopkins had won tenure at MIT at the young age of thirty-five, but from the beginning things didn't feel quite right.

She always felt that she had to battle for what she needed.

At one point, Hopkins was denied a request to add staff to her research group of twenty, even though most male tenured professors had average groups of twenty-three.

Later, she tested the waters again, this time spending "an exhausting year pleading with her superiors for an additional two hundred square feet of lab space, only to discover that even junior colleagues, many of them men, already had more space than she had."

Was there a pattern here?

She asked herself this question until 1994. Hopkins, by then fifty-seven, and a male colleague were teaching a biology course she had designed. When he informed her that he and another male professor were going to write a textbook based on her course material, her suspicions were confirmed.

But it wasn't until a woman who washed glassware in her lab turned to Hopkins and said "How come these men have so much and you have so little?" that she was prompted into taking the plunge.

NEVER TAKE A LEAP OF FAITH

Every move needs to be a measured stride, not a leap of faith. Unless you're an Olympic gold medal diver like Laura Wilkinson, jumping from a three-story-high platform might kill you.

I don't know how to swim. So for me, jumping into the deep end could be suicidal. Right now, "taking the plunge" means being in the guppy swimming class at the YMCA alongside a bunch of four-year-olds.

Do the research. Be brutally honest with yourself. Assess the risk, then decide what's right for you.

Following Dr. Hopkins's awakening, she decided to write a letter to the president of MIT.

Was she risking her job and perhaps her reputation? Of course. But she had tenure and was one of the most accomplished female scientists in the country. She knew she would recover.

Hopkins later told *Fast Company Magazine* that, as one final test of her decision, she "showed the letter to her most esteemed female colleague." To her surprise, the colleague not only thought it was the right thing to do but offered to co-sign the letter and join her when she met with the president.

"Sixteen of the university's seventeen tenured women in the sciences signed Hopkins's complaint," reports *Fast Company.*

With support from MIT President Charles Vest, the university listened, investigated the complaints, and has "redressed salary and space disparities."

What began as one woman's quest sparked a national movement. Today, women in science across the country are demanding the full opportunity to put their talents and gifts to work.

By carefully testing the waters, measuring her stride, and not taking a leap of faith, Dr. Hopkins has helped expand the pool of talent generating scientific breakthroughs.

BIG LEAPS

Did you know that in 1901 Anna Edison Taylor, a Michigan schoolteacher, became the first person—and the only woman—to survive going over Niagara Falls in a barrel? Now, I'm no daredevil. Just imagining that ride makes me nauseated, but even I admit that there are times when big leaps make sense.

The Internet revolution has helped make this possible. As we move from an industrial age to an information age, the world is spinning so fast that only gravity keeps us earthbound. Increasingly, we have to adapt to a world in which the old rules no longer apply.

Witness the difference technology has made for two women as diverse as Phyllis Street and Heidi Miller.

Street, an Appalachian coal miner's widow, recently took a headlong dive into the global economy. An expert quilter, she left her home on Virginia's Big A Mountain to travel to London, where her quilts were a star entry in the Ideal Home Show, Europe's premier craft exhibit. A grandmother who turned to quiltmaking as a matter of survival, Street now sells her one-of-a-kind works for $1,000 and more.

Using the Internet, planners in Appalachia market Street and other crafters at international shows around the world. Suddenly, cottage industries like quilting are becoming part of a growing export economy.

Despite her sheltered background, Street is embracing this venture, which honors her home region as much as her old-fashioned quilting techniques.

It's a big leap from Honaker, Virginia, to London, England, but Street was eager to make it. Her flight to London was the first plane trip of her life.

Heidi Miller took the leap from her perch as chief financial officer for Citigroup, with annual revenues of $60 billion, for the CFO spot at an Internet gamble, Priceline.com.

New York City–born, with a doctorate in Latin American history from Yale, Miller is not your typical CFO; she's a compulsive overachiever who worked through both her pregnancies.

"It's very powerful to walk into those meetings with a pregnant belly," she commented. "Men were so nervous that my water would break right there that I could hurry them to get things done."

Why did she take such a plunge? Because Priceline offered her "a seat at the table." And while this move turned out to be short-lived, she couldn't pass up the chance to run a business, an opportunity that might have eluded her had she stayed at Citigroup as a midcareer woman.

In an era of great flux, recycling old ideas and old moves is often insufficient. Take a stroll through the new landscape. You might find a big leap that makes sense for you.

NEVER DIVE WHEN
YOU'RE FEELING WEAK

Desperation is deadly! When you're feeling overwhelmed, exhausted, and beat, that's no time to make any kind of decision. But this is often when we are most willing to lie to ourselves, accept counterproductive behavior, and do dumb things.

Why? Because somewhere deep inside we recognize that if we're not coming to life we're dying. Our survival instinct gets activated, panic sets in, and we get hooked by some rescue fantasy.

Once I quit my father-in-law's firm, I found myself walking around in a mild state of shock. Where was the warm security blanket of my pension? What happened to that nice personnel lady who used to hand me a check that covered my mortgage and health insurance?

It's scary enough branching out on your own, but I had three rambunctious boys who had a habit of visiting the emergency room with their assorted injuries and whose college educations loomed in the distance like a mountain range.

I couldn't believe how exposed I felt. What if I couldn't swing this? What if I lost not only my shirt but everyone else's?

My company might have been manufacturing umbrellas, but there was nothing sheltering me. If it rained or the sun got too hot, I was going to get drenched or get burned.

I got both.

Clueless about the real workings of a business, I didn't know how to read a balance sheet or calculate my return on investment.

I lost money, floundered, blundered, and made a mess.

And I learned a cardinal rule about plunging: Never dive in out of weakness.

I discovered this at a point when I was dazed and bewildered in an entrepreneurial swampland of cash flow problems, personnel issues, supplier errors, and competitor ambushes. I had to be swift to avoid the alligators without falling into quicksand.

My life was a swarm of conflicting duties. I had three babies to care for and a household to manage; my husband, Steve, and I struggled with the business and how to manage our home life. And I was on the road a lot—flying from city to city, working to grow the company.

I became accustomed to pretzel lunches and airplane sandwich dinners; I learned to leave my suitcase on the bedroom floor because I would just have to drag it out again if I put it away.

Then one night I woke in another generic hotel room. I didn't even know what city I was in and actually had to check the card on the phone to determine my location.

Back home, I found my cell phone in the freezer one

morning. And I once took a diaper bag to the office instead of my briefcase.

Something had to give.

And then, on cue, just as I was feeling most like a damsel in distress, a man came galloping up my driveway.

He was a colleague I had known for years. Accomplished, strong, and sure of himself, he was eager to step in and help. He said all the right things: that he'd reduce my burden, take up the slack, and do some of the traveling so I could devote more time to my kids.

In my weakened state, this offer was irresistible.

Why not take the chance? I asked myself. *Why should I try to manage everything alone? Maybe I don't have to be superwoman anymore.*

All of this might have been true, but I was too exhausted to think it through with a clear head.

We drew up an employment agreement, and I naively handed this man my trust on a silver platter. I opened my books and gave him the inside scoop on my finances and my dreams. I took him around to meet my critical accounts and contacts. We lunched, strategized, and schmoozed.

I kept telling myself that it was going to work, even though there were niggling doubts in the back of my mind. But I made myself ignore them.

Trust, Deborah, you've got to learn to trust.

And so I tried.

Six months later, per our agreement, we sat down to look at his compensation structure. And at that meeting, he dropped the bomb.

"If you want me to stay, I'll do it for twenty-five percent of the business," he told me.

I was floored.

As I sat listening to him outline his demands, my whole working life flashed in front of me . . . from my pathetic typing job at NYU . . . to my stint in the Lyndhurst, New Jersey, Parks and Recreation Department . . . to my staggering into the office weeks after my C-sections to check on accounts. Each of those steps had brought me to where I was today, and if this guy thought I was giving a quarter of that away, he was out of his mind!

I wrote him a severance check and showed him the door.

And I knew I alone had created this mess. I took him on as part of a rescue fantasy that I reverted to because I was feeling desperate and weak.

Now, when I leap, I make sure it's from a position of strength.

USE DISAPPOINTMENTS TO LIGHT THE WAY

After this setback, I had to regain my footing.

It took time, but slowly and surely I got back to making my business a success—on my own terms. Yet even as I was prospering, there were ways in which I was keeping myself safe and holding back.

I had the look of success but not the feel of it—I might have appeared sleek and sophisticated in my designer clothes, but no one could see my threadbare interior.

I kept tallying up the reasons I should be happy, and there were plenty of them. I was the CEO of a growing enterprise, a company of terrific employees who had great ideas. Except for the occasional call from their principal about a fistfight, my three sons were thriving. I had a beautifully decorated home in a perfectly landscaped setting right outside San Francisco.

As I surveyed my accomplishments, I kept saying, *You did this, Deborah: the terrazzo tiled pool, the cathedral ceilings, the fine car . . . it's all because of you!*

I deeply appreciated every diamond I wore, every lobster I ate, every perk for my kids. But it wasn't enough.

What's the matter with you? I kept asking myself. *If this isn't the fulfillment of the American dream for a girl from the South Bronx who started out without a dime to her name, then what is?*

It might have been the American dream, but it wasn't *my* dream. . . .

I was grateful for every single thing I had. But being grateful isn't the same thing as being satisfied.

You can't bully yourself into fulfillment.

What's *supposed* to make you happy is irrelevant.

Each of us has a unique reason for being on this planet.

There's no one-size-fits-all destiny, like a muumuu that fits every woman.

You can bury your reason for existence or ignore it at your own risk, but trying to fashion it to fit someone else's expectations is a colossal waste of energy and time.

I saw that a life of acquiring trinkets wasn't going to do it for me.

Being remembered as the umbrella lady wasn't going to be enough, either.

This sunny life had nothing to do with my deepest

desires, but I couldn't even articulate what they were. I just
knew that I wanted more. I knew I needed to test the waters
and build meaningful relationships. But I'd played this way
so long I wasn't sure how to stop.

Even though I was orchestrating the growth of my business, I'd remained a shadowy figure, without identity or
gender. I'd remained closeted in the background of my own
enterprise, letting seasoned older men represent my company out in the world. Most of my vendors and customers
had no idea that there was a young Hispanic mother of three
running the show. And that was just as I'd intended.

Often, at a trade show, customers would come up to the
booth, ask me for literature, then wait to speak to one of the
men.

In a pre–Ricky Martin world, I became known as Deborah Shaw, disguising myself with my husband's American-
ized name just as his Jewish relatives had disguised
themselves when they immigrated to America.

I'd stuffed all the spunk and flare of the Rosados behind
a generic, homogenized label. I'd thought this would keep
people focused on the product instead of on who I was, and
it had worked. But it also began to have an impact on my
psyche. I felt that my life was an elaborate masquerade and I
was never going to get the chance to tear off the mask. Even
worse, I sometimes *forgot* that I was even wearing a mask. I
began to feel trapped behind my own false front. There
were times when I saw myself in the mirror and wondered
Who is that woman?

One afternoon, in the middle of a stuffy banker's meeting, I had an almost uncontrollable urge to burst into Spanish. And sometimes at night I yearned to throw open the

windows of our sedate suburban house and play salsa music at full blast.

What was happening to me?

DO SOME SOUL-SEARCHING

In the middle of this turmoil, I was notified that my brother, Josh, had been admitted to a New York hospital in one of his worst medical crises ever.

When Josh was fourteen, my father had donated one of his kidneys in an attempt to save his son's life. It had worked—but for nine years Josh's body had been slowly rejecting this transplant.

There's no way to live without a kidney. If Josh lost it, he'd have to go on dialysis to survive.

I flew in on a red-eye from California to be with my brother. My parents and I alternated staying at his side overnight.

At home and at work, I was so harried, so pulled in a hundred directions, that it was almost a relief to find this one place where I knew I truly belonged.

One evening, as I sat beside my brother's bed, I looked over at his slender body, strung with tubes and IVs. By then Josh had already undergone three operations in a vain attempt to save the kidney. My parents and I might have been near him, but in so many ways this was his solitary fight.

As he looked over at me with his tired smile, I wondered where he got his strength. I felt small beside him.

As soon as he drifted off to sleep, I wandered out into the hall. On one hand, I was terrified to leave his bedside, worried that he might slip away while I wasn't there. On the other, I was so wired up with tension and worry that I found it impossible to sit still.

That night, as I paced the hospital's corridors, I overheard an exchange between a female physician and a couple who were huddled together in a hallway.

"There must be a mistake," the husband was saying as I approached them.

"No," the doctor insisted. "I've told you before. There's no doubt. This is a definitive diagnosis."

The doctor's voice grew increasingly exasperated as I drew near.

She said, "Listen, I can't wait any longer for you to face the fact that your baby has leukemia. You *must* sign this consent for treatment or I'll get a court order to save her."

I was close enough to see the couple's blank and terrified faces.

The wife shook her head and the husband tightened his lips. They were obviously so immobilized by denial that they couldn't do the very thing that might save their child.

By the time I returned to my brother's darkened room, I was shaking. The exchange in the hall had struck me like an arrow in the heart. Those strangers had forced me to come face-to-face with my own denial and blindness.

I went to the window and looked out at the night while my brother labored to breathe behind me.

As I stood there, I felt *time* in that room as if it were a force of nature. I had no idea how much more of it Josh would have . . . or I.

I made myself see what I didn't want to see—that I had made a secret agreement with myself to settle for less.

I was going to have to change my life.

But how could I do this?
I had no idea.

FOLLOW YOUR GUT

The only thing I knew for sure was I had a persistent feeling that I needed to move back east.

It might have been beautiful right outside San Francisco, but it was so far from New York and Washington that I felt I was on the margins of my business world. I missed industry events because I didn't want to be away from my sons. Instead of expanding my opportunities, living there was holding me back.

This gut feeling was the only sure thing I had, so I held on to it for dear life. I kept testing the waters. I made countless trips to the East Coast, tabulated the number of trade events I could attend and still be home for dinner, listed the number of accounts I would have greater contact with, and asked God for "signs" that this was the right move.

Against the advice of everyone I knew, I began to completely redesign my enterprise and life and made plans to move to New Jersey. And, just in case, I started to cozy up to the headhunters I used to ignore.

My kids were pissed off at me. My husband said, grudgingly, "If you really want to do this, go ahead." But I knew that whatever went wrong would be my fault.

My mentor, joined by my accountant, asked, "Deborah, what are you running from?"

And all I could say was, "I'm not running from, but to."

I'd been perched at the edge of big decisions so many times; but this one was different. This was the first decision

I'd made based on what *I* needed, knowing that it would impact my whole family, especially my kids.

I kept praying for clarity, but what I really wanted was insurance that everything would work out, that I wouldn't hurt anyone, that I wouldn't look stupid, that my kids wouldn't hate me.

But no one sold such a policy.

I continued to wade through the murky questions in my life: *Am I worth it? Do I have the right to want so much? Could I give myself permission to dream big?*

And the only reply I heard was a tepid "Maybe."

LIFE IS MESSY! BEWARE THE MURKY WATERS

In the background of this move was my search for neat answers to complex questions. For years my husband and I had been struggling to have the kind of marriage we both desperately wanted. We had tried everything—crying, yelling, fighting, counseling—without success. We both knew our marriage was on life support, but we just couldn't bear to pull the plug. As Gladys Knight sang, "Neither one of us wants to be the first to say good-bye."

Food became my comfort, my secret midnight companion. Late at night, I'd stand in the cool light of the refrigerator and try to fill the bottomless pit of my terror with bread and chocolate and cheese.

As I stuffed myself, I'd wonder: *Why aren't you satisfied? How far can you go in one generation? How much can a divorced woman with three kids do?*

With time it became clear that Steve and I were at the

edge of the cliff of our life in California. Below us churned the murky waters of unknown depths.

How could we take three kids we both adored and our own continuing love for each other and make our relationship function in a new way?

In my panic, I tried to think of every possible way to get off that cliff without getting into the dark, choppy water.

But I knew what I had to do.

So I held my nose and took the plunge.

God help me was my thought.

PUMMELED BY TIDAL WAVES

Just as I'd feared, all heck broke loose once I hit New Jersey, and I had to face the chaos I'd created.

I felt guilty about the people I'd had to lay off in California. I felt terrible about shoving my family's life into a hundred boxes. I had to pay back a huge line of credit, settle legal items with my former partners, stabilize a spooked sales force, and rebuild my business. All while presenting a cool mask to my customers and business associates.

I found myself sitting all day in an empty New Jersey office, answering phones and soothing customers, then returning home at night to a houseful of unhappy sons, who met me at the door crying, "We hate it here!"

It felt as if I were holding the steering wheel steady on the way to a crash.

The upheaval left me filled with self-doubt. I began to wonder, *What was I reaching for? Why wasn't I satisfied with what I had?*

Then, like millions of women before me who have felt alone and overwhelmed, I sank like a rock into depression.

That move from California to New Jersey was the beginning of a three-thousand-mile journey back to myself.

But it took a long while for me to know that.

I'd hoped I could quit swimming once I reached the East Coast, but I bobbed around in those waves for months.

I followed my internal sonar into uncharted waters, and when I wasn't struggling against the tide, I was floating in exhaustion.

Little did I know that I'd just begun the swim of my life.

DECISIONS, DECISIONS, DECISIONS

If you want access to what's possible in life you'll have to make many tough decisions. And no, you can't have it all. But you can have something.

When we watch or read about women who have taken the plunge, the process they used to prepare for the jump is rarely revealed. We're never told the intimate conversations they have with themselves, the questions asked, alternatives considered.

I've had the privilege of speaking to thousands and thousands of women all over the country and in so doing learning about their stories, challenges, and triumphs. I've identified some of the common steps that transform ordinary gals into brave and bold women. Following is some of their best advice:

- ◆ **Listen to your discontent** and be brutally honest with yourself about where it's coming from.

- **Challenge your assumptions** and dare to make new conclusions. Dare to throw away the old and try on something different. You might like the fit.
- **Test the waters** and prepare to be uncomfortable. Cold waters won't kill you as long as you're not in over your head.
- **Probe the alternatives** to quiet the discontent with the least disruption possible.
- **Take baby steps,** small incremental actions that grow in boldness and confirm your assessments. It's so much fun to look back and say, "I was right! See there, I was *right!*"
- **Take the plunge** and get ready to give birth to a new future—often in your current relationship or with your current employer, and sometimes in a new relationship, new company, or new career.

Each of these successful women tests, measures, and considers in her own way. Often, they ask God for signs or even try to force a decision by having someone else make it for them. But as they sit on the edge of what is and what isn't, their soul-searching questions are probably the same as yours and mine. They, too, ask themselves:

- Why do I feel this way?
- Why can't I be satisfied?
- How do I know this is what I really want?
- Am I settling, or am I asking for too much?
- What if I fail?
- What will people think?
- What if I look stupid?
- Is it worth it?

See, you *do* have something in common (probably many things) with these dynamic ladies. *Everyone* has doubts. Unlike a professional chess game, life has no buzzers to go off and tell you it's your turn. And some of us will spend countless years between moves.

Bring back a moment when you felt really alive, when time stood still enough to notice the rise and fall of your chest and the blood pumping through your veins. An instance of letting yourself feel bigger than your own might and stature. A connection to your greater purpose.

If you haven't had this moment, go and fetch one, because this is where the answers lie. Answers unique to you alone.

BLOOPERS WELCOME HERE

Don't expect to look good or be smart all of the time. Actually, if you're really living you'll have plenty of moments of looking stupid and feeling dumb.

Take a look at Joan Rivers. If ever there was a "Bounce-back Queen," she's it. Humiliated by the cancellation of her talk show, a TV boycott, an estrangement from her only child, financial ruin, and the shocking suicide of her husband, Edgar—today Joan is regularly joined on E! by her daughter, Melissa, and has become the Grande Dame of Jewelry on QVC.

I've had plenty of gutter-roaming moments myself. I've trusted harmful people, hired the wrong folk, lost money, made stupid agreements, and fallen flat on my face . . . in public.

So, how do you go from "Why me?" to "What's next?"*

The trick is to stand in those moments remembering this: *If you're willing to lose some, you stand to gain lots.*

From Lucille Ball to Elizabeth Dole to Ellen DeGeneres, they've all been there, done that.

Gutter balls can't kill you; they just don't score you any points.

SUFFERING IS OPTIONAL

Now I know, some of us are really into suffering: *Woe is me! Why do these things happen to me? What have I done wrong? Why can't I have so-and-so's life?* You wouldn't let yourself move to the bright side even if your life depended on it.

And guess what? It does.

I've been there, and I want you to know that suffering is a choice.

Often, despair is a by-product of having experienced a moment of your own self-greatness, then turning away from it.

If you find yourself sitting in misery for long periods of time, you're collecting some dividend that somehow makes it worthwhile for you.**

Maybe you won't have to experience your full beauty.

Maybe you won't have to learn what you're really capable of.

*The title of a talk I heard once given by Paul Ratzlaff.

**You might also need professional help. Clinical depression is an illness that can be treated with medication. You wouldn't think of mending a broken bone yourself; don't try it here, either.

Maybe you won't have to leave others behind.

Your most desperate and heartfelt dream might be one you convinced yourself a long time ago you could never really have. Or maybe you're holding on to a dream that died ages ago.

Make a thorough examination of your life, your job, your relationships, your dreams, and ask yourself this important question:

If I had three years to live, where and how would I spend the rest of me?

When you begin to truly understand what brings meaning to *your* life, you'll start taking risks that are appropriate and effective.

Chapter 10

Dream Big! And Live It Now

"You are the architect of your own life."

—Diane Dreher

I'm going to let you in on a little secret—we are all free to choose and create our lives.

Then why don't we do it?

Because we're scared and because we're lazy.

When we realize we have choices, a load of work shows up. And this is work of a different kind than figuring profit and loss or returns on investment, or landing that promotion. You might think it's heavy lifting—deep internal work, the kind most of us would rather avoid.

Once you accept the idea that you are born full of potential and that you're also born with the power to fully express that potential, the entire illusion we live under—that we're helpless pawns in a predetermined game—is exposed.

And then we have to deal with the questions that realization produces:

- ◆ Why am I here?
- ◆ Does my life have a purpose?
- ◆ How can I live a life of few or no regrets?
- ◆ What is possible?

LISTEN TO THE WHISPERS OF GOD

After transplanting my family and my business to the East Coast, I assumed both would quickly thrive and blossom. But I must admit, we took a while to take root, and for a time we were a droopy, wilted bunch. I kept hoping for divine intervention, that celestial whisper in my ear giving me clear directions, or even an encouraging "Atta girl! You did the right thing!"

Along with some clear instructions, I wanted my reward for making a bold move and taking on the heat. But it was a long time coming.

Meanwhile, I forced myself to perform the heroic acts of getting out of bed in the morning and placing one sore foot in front of the next. Not very dramatic, but sometimes that's all there was to do. Instinctively, I knew that if I persisted, surely and steadily, I would eventually live my dream.

But, having taken the "big plunge," I wasn't sure where to go next. I needed direction, but there were no blinking neon arrows pointing the way.

I was to discover that divine guidance is seldom so flashy.

The world screams at us with its roadside billboards, radio commercials, news broadcasts, and a constant barrage of dictatorial commands—cleverly disguised as gentle, well-meaning advice—issued by friends, relatives, and co-workers. But, like the soft voice of your own inner spirit, "God" sometimes speaks in whispers.

The universe can communicate with the human heart by using something as simple as a line of poetry, the unexpected beauty of a sunset, the notes of a haunting melody, a proverb embroidered on a pillow . . . or even a crumpled bit of trash.

Sitting at my desk in New Jersey, feeling lost, wishing for that neon direction indicator, I found a tiny piece of crunched paper clinging to the underside of my blotter, having survived a three-thousand-mile move. This bit of "garbage" was a notice that I had plucked out of a magazine months earlier in California. It described the Avon Women of Enterprise Award co-sponsored by the U.S. Small Business Administration.

Sitting there at my desk, with that piece of paper in my hand, I heard a whisper. I felt the fire that had been lying like banked embers deep in my belly stir, then reignite. It wasn't a flashing arrow, but in some way it spoke just as clearly to my heart.

So I wrote the required essays, provided the necessary biographical info, and sent it in.

And then I went back to the humdrum of "real" life: piles of laundry, paperwork, board meetings, phone messages, grocery shopping, and basketball practices.

Until one morning when I spotted an envelope in the middle of the credit card bills and junk mail. The return address read, Avon Products.

I opened the envelope and almost fainted. The letter inside read: "We're pleased to inform you that you've been selected a winner of the 1996 Avon Women of Enterprise Award."

Needless to say, I was extremely thankful for the subtle direction I had been given by that scrap of paper stuck to my blotter. I had listened to the whisper, followed my heart, and would receive what I was sure would be a pleasant little award. How nice. I imagined a modest award ceremony with a buffet lunch and maybe a plaque for my wall.

But this award was far bigger than that.

YOU ARE NEVER ALONE

Early on the day of the awards luncheon, I went to the ballroom to check out the space and get a feel for the stage. As I stood taking in the lofty ceilings and grand chandeliers, watching hotel staff scurry around setting up tables and arranging silverware, I was simply overwhelmed.

Staring out beyond the rows and rows of tables to the back of the ballroom, the most amazing thing happened. I saw an image of two women: one was on her knees with a bucket and rag; the other was bent over a sewing machine.

Looking right back at me were the struggles of my paternal grandmother and my maternal great-grandmother, both of whom had left behind children and homes in Puerto Rico in order to pursue a brighter future for their families in New York—one in a garment sweatshop and the other in this very hotel, the Waldorf-Astoria.

It was hard to believe that Mama Juanita had worked on

her knees in the very building where her great-granddaughter would now stand in a place of honor.

My grandmothers' lives had been back-breaking and lonely. They'd lived in tenements, unable to speak English, without the warmth and security of their birthplace. They'd both risked everything to provide a better life for their children. And all of my life I'd stood on the shoulders of these brave women—and the many before them who'd worked hard, without any idea how their efforts might affect future generations.

They were a part of the patchwork quilt of who I was. These women had anchored and supported me even when I hadn't realized it.

If they could confront their worst fears and accomplish so much with so little, the least I owed them was to honor their memory and do my best.

TRUTH IS POWERFUL

Walking past Joan Rivers and Professor Davidson, with my sons, parents, and business associates looking on, I delivered the first true speech of my life. I stood at the podium, my heart beating a syncopated song. I shared my full story, my *real* story, not a sanitized version.

In doing so, I came to terms with where I had come from and where I was going. In embracing my own history, I was connecting to a story far larger than myself.

That day I came out of the closet as myself, Deborah Rosado Shaw, one of a long line of strong and courageous women.

As I spoke, I felt my sources of shame being put to rest—getting knocked into the mud and called a spic, feeling the man in the church creeping up behind me. The roaches, the rats, the fear in the night . . . I didn't bury them, but they took their place in the fabric of my life.

I hardly knew what words I said, just that they were true, as if I were having a long conversation with myself. And when I finished, I couldn't believe my ears—thunderous applause from people who were visibly moved.

In that moment, I saw the power of standing in your truth, and it changed my life.

SPEAK YOUR DREAM OUT LOUD

Words are the form through which you can will *things to life.* First you must acknowledge the dream to yourself. Then you must speak it out loud, where it counts and where people will answer your call to bring it to life.

In my acceptance speech I made a statement that surprised even me: "I hope someday to survive three teenage sons and write a best-selling book."

From the time I was a girl, whenever something unbelievable happened to me, even if it was painful, I filed it away in my mind and thought, *I've got to remember this! I've got to tell this to someone!*

When I walked by the dead body in front of our church, when I met with the dreadful dean at Wellesley, when I ascended the stairs of the American Museum of Natural History, I tried to etch the details in my memory.

I knew these things had happened for a reason but I hadn't yet discovered why.

Until that speech.

As I spoke, I thought, *If I can make it through all my dark times and emerge on the other side, that means somebody else can, too, and she just doesn't know it yet. Maybe I can help her.*

After my speech I was surrounded by a crowd of well-wishers, including an elegant woman I'd never seen before. She waited patiently at the back of the crowd and finally came up to me, extending her hand.

"I'm an editor at Simon and Schuster," she said. "If you're serious about writing that book, give me a call." And she handed me her card.

I couldn't have been more shocked if a fairy godmother had materialized with a wand. It was only one more amazing part of that storybook day.

I took her card with a smile and said to myself, *Tomorrow, Deborah, you'll wake up.*

DON'T UNDERESTIMATE YOUR REACH

Many times I had read the words "What you speak, you live." But I had never experienced it in quite this way.

The real shock came the morning after the awards ceremony, when I returned to real life with a dull thud. I was exhausted, my kids were hungry, and the dog had run away one more time. I caught my reflection in the toaster oven, eyes like a raccoon's, ringed with yesterday's mascara.

I was in the kitchen, surrounded by math homework and hockey sticks, making peanut butter sandwiches, when I heard the faxes forwarded from my office inching out of the machine.

With a knife in one hand, I went into my home office and pulled out the faxes. On top was a note from the Simon and Schuster editor.

As if in answer to an unspoken question in my head, it read: "I was moved by the ease and power of your presentation. If you're really serious about that book, I'd be very interested in talking with you."

There in the light of day, standing barefoot with peanut butter on my hands, it hit me even harder than the day before. *This was real.*

In the days that followed, I had to absorb the astounding turn my life had taken.

To ascend from the pits of Prozac to the accolades of strangers was disorienting. It was a shock to my perceived limitations. I had to accept the fact that I'd been dreaming way too small.

For a while, I kept expecting to snap awake and end up back in my hesitant life, but it didn't happen. Instead, as the days passed, more doors swung open.

I was bombarded with requests: speaking engagements, articles to write, television interviews, magazine features, parties, and events of all kinds.

KEEP LISTENING

Of course, we all want evidence that we're on the right track. And I needed *lots* of it.

With the business growing in leaps and bounds and the boys having more and more of a social life, I kept thinking,

Where will I find the time to take on one more huge project?

And besides, I didn't know anything about writing or selling a book; who was I kidding?

When my business coach, Pat Miller, offered me some encouraging words, I said, "From your mouth to God's ears." And she replied, "No, Deborah, it's from God's mouth to your ears." She urged me to keep looking—and, most important, to keep listening. The answers would come.

So I made a deal with the universe. I said, "Listen, if this book thing is really something I should be doing, I'm gonna need some BIG signs . . . preferably in neon."

NEON SIGNS

I decided to accept a few speaking engagements to see if what I had to say had any relevance to people outside New York. From Fargo, North Dakota, to St. Cloud, Minnesota, to Kansas City, Missouri, I flew all over the country to see for myself.

As my words were embraced by roomfuls of strangers, standing and clapping, I saw how much my truth-telling meant to others, how they identified with my troubles and triumphs, and how that connection inspired us all.

Their encouragement taught me that although we might seem different on the exterior we are 99 percent the same. We worry for our children, struggle for our families, and pray for the world. And we each yearn for love, validation, and meaning.

These women—and yes, men, too—from all over the country helped me realize that my story represented more than my own life, that I represented something larger than myself.

And then, one day, I felt strong enough to pick up the phone and call the Simon and Schuster editor.

Which is when the journey to this book really began.

MY ROAD HERE

For most of my life I've felt like a girl playing pin the tail on the donkey—occasionally blindfolded by doubt and fear but getting warmer all the time. And with every win I grew stronger and more determined.

I kept letting go of the heavy bags of fear, anger, and guilt I'd been dragging behind me. And I slowly began to glimpse the payoff for all the moves I'd made in terror and blindness.

I saw that, as if I were the heroine in an adventure story, I'd been on a quest, and the destination had been *myself.*

First I dared to peek from under my mask and say to myself, *This is who I am!* Then I said the same thing to my children.

And what a wonderful surprise! My world didn't disintegrate. The sun rose the next morning; my kids ate cereal at the breakfast table.

And I said to myself, *Huh, look at that!*

So I kept moving. And I remained in action even when I wasn't sure where I was headed. I tried to keep my eye on the destination at the top of the hill while staying aware of the surprises that glittered on the side of the road. If there was a wall with a stop sign on it, I climbed over it or found a way to knock it down.

Whenever I came upon a woman I admired, I tried to emulate her and extend a grateful hand to those crowding behind me.

I formed alliances that could sustain me and others.

And then, when I felt strong enough, I took the plunge, telling the people of the world my story, showing them who I really was. A self was emerging whom I barely knew, a woman who loved herself, a woman full of conviction and purpose.

The feisty girl I'd been was joining hands with the committed adult. All my selves finally joined together in a circle.

IT'S YOUR TURN

Take a good look at the stories in this book. Neither Nancy nor Aubyn nor Mercedes nor Rose was born with anything special. No caped crusaders here. No genetic predisposition to anything magnificent. They're just ordinary people living extraordinary lives.

And you can, too, if you so choose.

Whoever you are, whatever your circumstances, you have choices. And you can impact the world around you—at your kitchen table, in your company's boardroom, or on the international political stage—with the choices you make.

The question is: Will you?

"Why Do I Feel So Scared?"

Remember how you felt when you first learned that Santa wasn't real? What other lies had you been told? What other assumptions in your life might not be true?

We tend to cling to all our long-held fantasies, whether they are stories of Saint Nick, tales about the Easter Bunny, or negative falsehoods about our own inadequacies. It is difficult to release deeply ingrained lies from your psyche, but you must if you are ever going to achieve your dreams.

One of the worse falsehoods is the idea that there is some "magic" that endows certain people with access to their dreams but denies that access to others. We tend to think that these people are different from ourselves, that they were born with special characteristics. They were somehow plucked from among the rest of us, we believe, set aside by some unseen force and predestined for greatness. Lucky them!

But it isn't so. They are just people, no different from anyone else except that they have made choices and taken the necessary steps to create the extraordinary lives they live.

And a world like theirs—or, even better, one of your own design—is just as available to you if you're willing to make your own choices and take your own steps.

That's the good news. The bad news is that no giant tornado is going to appear out of the Kansas sky and sweep you away to your Land of Oz. If you are going to live your dreams, and you absolutely can, you are going to have to make it happen. And that's where all the work comes in.

Because it's easier and far less frightening, we generally agree to settle for less than what's possible, to simply allow life to happen to us, rather than to make *us* happen to life.

And why do we accept this lie that says we can't realize our dreams because we aren't among the lucky chosen few? Because preconceived notions, no matter how ugly, untrue, and harmful, are familiar, and therefore comfortable. So it's no wonder that after years of denying our birthright to greatness, we feel frightened when this fact is exposed.

But, scary or not, the truth is: We've all had access to our dreams all along.

Once this new truth finds its way into your heart, you'll be on your way to living an extraordinary life.

"Why Can't I Move?"

Just about the time you decide to really move forward, that scared feeling is compounded by overwhelming bouts of laziness. Why? Because moving forward looks like so much work. Contemplating what appear to be monumental decisions about what to do and who to do it with, we settle into spectator mode. Sitting back, we become extras in the movie of our life, existing simply to support somebody else's story line.

Although mediocrity might not be very fulfilling or exciting, it is easy and comfortable—and therefore addicting. Once we become hooked on maintaining the status quo, we must lie to ourselves, assuring ourselves that we can't have our innermost desires.

The very word *excellence* implies an enormous amount of work and self-discipline, not to mention challenges that we feel incompetent to meet. The whole idea is so threatening that we often behave in counterproductive ways and accept less than we deserve.

Why do we do this? Is it because we don't really want more? No. Our souls yearn for full self-expression. But deep inside, where our truth lies, we know that we can't do it alone. It's just too big a job for anyone.

No one can do it alone. No one ever has.

And the good news is: You don't have to, either.

You've no doubt heard the old adage "God helps those

who help themselves." And while this is usually uttered in a cynical, caustic tone, aimed at people the speaker considers to be slackers, the words are true and quite beautiful. Take a few steps on your own behalf, and you will be amazed at how many blessings come, unbidden, your way. Problems dissolve, opportunities rise, and resources materialize in ways that you never imagined. Start walking, even stumbling, down the right path, and you will be met . . . more than halfway.

So, if the possibility of bringing your innermost passions to life sounds like an awesome, overwhelming task, and you feel a wave of fear or laziness coming on, just remember that help is on its way. Instead of being a pitcher that runs dry with outpouring—you will find that you become a channel through which life-giving energy flows.

What Must You Do?

If you want to satisfy the hunger for a life that's filled with joy and vitality, you must seek your purpose.

Each of us has one, and when we are aligned with it, we become unstoppable.

Whether you're stuck, hesitating, or barreling really fast down a slick road—your purpose won't come to you gift-wrapped and tied in a golden ribbon.

For each of us the answer is different. And you must go out and seek yours.

There is a lot more to answering this question than a simple: *What will I be when I grow up someday?* We aren't talking about the endless decisions concerning occupation, number of children, or whether or not the picket fence will be white.

I'm talking about deciding who you're going to be for yourself—from this moment forward.

I'm talking about deciding to explore every gift, use your passion, and not settle.

One way to explore this issue is to determine what really matters to you. Sit down with a pen and paper and write yourself a eulogy. I know, it sounds a bit morbid. Most of us are a little queasy about even putting together a will. But macabre aspects aside, think about what you would want said about you. If you could "sum up" your life in a few hundred words, what would you want those sentences to say?

What were your major accomplishments?
Whose life did you impact?
Where did you go?
Whom did you love?
Who loved you?

Would you want your eulogy to say that you were a devoted parent, a faithful spouse, a principled businessperson? Maybe you would want your eulogy to mention the ways you had served your community over the years, the gifts you had given, your efforts to ease suffering and brighten the lives of others. How will you be remembered?

When you look back, you probably won't regret what you did or didn't do; you'll most likely regret the person you failed to be: courageous, joyful, powerful, bold, compassionate. Whatever you would want said is probably what is dearest to your heart.

Who must you be in life?

If you figure out who you must *be,* you'll discover what you must *do.*

MAKE A COMMITMENT

One of the first things you must do is make a commitment. Commitments aren't about convenience. They're about honoring yourself and the privilege of life you've been given.

When you commit to fulfilling your purpose, you commit to leaving this world with your potential to learn, to love, and to create completely used up. And if you promise to live this way, day in and day out, there will be no stopping you.

And you can start right now. You don't have to know what your purpose is before you begin. Your commitment itself will provide the knowledge.

Where to Start

1. Take a Vow

Promise yourself to live a powerful life by fulfilling your purpose: I, _____, promise to fulfill my purpose. Every day, when you wake, remind yourself of the person you've promised to be.

2. Stand Up and Be Counted

Use your talents and strengths. Maybe you can cook, or write poetry, or sing, or soothe the sick, or make people laugh. Whatever your talents, they were given to you for a reason. By using them, you will receive a transfusion of energy . . . the power of creativity in its purest form.

Consider the following questions:

Where have you been holding yourself back?
Where are you settling?

What do you have to say, to contribute?
What is your passion?
Where can you make a difference?

3. Examine Your Truth

Painful, joyful, dark days and bright, your experiences are yours alone. No one else has lived your life. Every trauma, every success, has taught you something. Sit down and write the story of your life. What circumstances, good and bad, shaped who you are? What themes appear? What were the turning points? What were the life-altering moments?

What if every single thing in your life—your talents, experiences, virtues, and vices; your patchwork of relatives and friends—had a purpose? What would that purpose be?

DREAM BIG

When ordinary people dare to Dream BIG! they gain access to greatness. Fueled by their dream, they find meaning and discover their own purpose.

Where to Start

1. Shoot for the Stars

Create a dream big enough that its might will act like a magnetic force drawing you forward, through, and around whatever obstacles or hurdles might appear.

2. Pick Something Delicious

It doesn't really matter what it is, as long as you keep taking the steps. Whether it's being the best mom your children could have, guiding at-risk young people to find their way, finding a cure for breast cancer, having a job that expresses all of your talents, appearing on the cover of *Fortune*—what dream beckons you, moves you, inspires you, and maybe even scares you?

3. Speak Your Dream Out Loud

If you want to connect with a force field greater than you, you're gonna have to tell somebody what you're up to. Declare your ambition and be prudent about where you do it and with whom. Start where it's safest, then graduate to where it counts.

4. Don't Relinquish Your Dreams to Your Circumstances

Dream BIG! doesn't mean you'll have smaller challenges. Every journey follows a meandering path with dips and curves, delays and roadblocks. And no there are no guarantees that things will turn out as *you've* planned. But when the obstacles appear, remind yourself of who you've promised to be in life.

SURRENDER

Get out of your own way. This is no time to be stubborn or positional. Some of us are so attached to our ideas of what *should be* or *will be* that we keep driving up the road marked "Wrong Way." And then we insist on doing it over and over again.

Where to Start

1. Stop Struggling

If you're struggling too hard, you might be doing the wrong thing. At some point it should become effortless—not that there's no hard work, just that there's no hard effort.

2. It's Not All Up to You

Your strength alone will never be enough. When you are seeking your purpose, all sorts of unplanned, unexpected, unanticipated happenings will occur. Expect miracles, coincidences, and breakthroughs as long as you keep taking those steps.

3. Let Your Intuition Guide You

Listen to your heart and your spirit. Listen to your energy. Notice when you come alive, feel most vibrant. That's where your purpose lies.

- Are you listening to the whispers of God?
- Are you ignoring the messages that are trying to show you the way?
- Where do you keep running into a brick wall?
- Where have miracles taken place?
- Have you noticed the angels sent to help?
- What doors have opened?
- What doors have closed?

LIVE IT NOW!

So how do *you* live it now?

You shouldn't depend on achieving your dreams in order to find happiness and fulfillment, because you might never get to where you think you're going.

Living it now is about having a soulful journey, a journey of self-discovery during which you can feel the chords of your life being played. And when they are played you become an instrument of God and all things powerful.

Everything I had been searching for was right under my nose. I was born good enough, perfect, with nothing to make up for, strive for, or prove . . . and so were you! We come equipped with everything we need to experience a powerful life full of great joy, incredible passion, endless creativity, and profound peace.

The question is whether or not we'll allow ourselves to live it.

The more I understood this, the more I surrendered.

I knew something was really changing when, instead of being angry for the injustices in life—particularly my brother's grueling struggle—I started to look for ways to be grateful.

I began to appreciate all the years my brother had lived beyond the doctors' best hopes, the opportunity to have him love my children and them love him, the courage I've been privileged to witness, and the teacher he has been for me.

The more I surrendered, the more I began to experience a shift. In the midst of a bomb scare at my son's high school, three sons in simultaneous puberty, my endometriosis, a divorce, the news that a distant cousin had shot himself in the head, my mother's cancer and loww of sight from glaucoma, my sister's challenge with her severely injured husband, my brother's fight for life, and our beloved Grandma Eli's passing, I still continue to find peace.

Be led by your dream, but be free of expectation. To live it now, you've got to be in the Dream BIG! game as much for the adventure as for the goal.

EXPERIENCE YOUR GREATNESS

What if *all* human beings could experience their greatness, live their purpose, and leave with their potential fully exhausted? What kind of a world would that create?

Ask yourself: *What does my life make possible? Who could I be for myself, my family, my community, my organization, my company, the world?*

What future could you imagine where you would:

- Claim your power
- Stop fighting fear
- Make bold moves
- Get focused
- Build a powerful network
- Take something or somebody on
- Play beyond the rules
- Build a winning portfolio
- Move through the obstacles
- Take the plunge

What purpose could use up every ounce of your potential?

As you ponder these questions and move through the an-

swers, consider the following words, written by Marianne
Williamson in her book *A Return to Love*.

> *Our deepest fear is not that we are inadequate.*
> *Our deepest fear*
> *is that we are powerful beyond measure.*
> *It is our light, not our darkness*
> *that most frightens us.*
> *We ask ourselves, who am I to be brilliant,*
> *gorgeous, talented, and fabulous?*
> *Actually, who are you not to be?*
> *You are a child of God.*
> *Your playing small doesn't serve the world.*
> *There is nothing enlightened about shrinking*
> *so that other people*
> *won't feel insecure around you.*
> *We were born to make manifest*
> *the glory of God that is within us.*
> *It's not just in some of us; it's in everyone*
> *and as we let our own light shine,*
> *We unconsciously give other people*
> *permission to do the same.*
> *As we are liberated from our own fear,*
> *our presence automatically liberates others.*

Remember, there is only one of *you* in the history of
time—one person with *your* particular story, *your* particular
circumstances, *your* challenges and lessons.

Take your chance.

Sing your song.

Make your mark.

Today is the best day and now is the best time.

Use *you* well.

Acknowledgments

THIS BOOK IS THE result of an incredible journey fueled by the love, support, and guidance I received from countless people.

My deepest thanks to my agent and friend Rusty Robertson who believed in me from day one. Your powerful commitment, boundless energy, and warrior strength were the rock I leaned on to bring this book to life. You are an extraordinary woman.

And my deepest thanks to Lynn Lauber, who hung in there when everything said quit and who lent her life experiences and talent to help me tell my story.

My warm thanks to Sonja Massie for her incredible spirit and guidance throughout this project. You asked the right questions, encouraged me to trust my words, and made me laugh at just the right moments.

To Dominick Anfuso, thank you for taking this project on. Your trust and guiding hand made all the difference. To the Dream BIG publishing team, Bill Shinker, Suzanne Donahue, Carisa Hays, and Jenny Dworkin, thank you for seeing the possibility and working to bring it to life. And my gratitude to Rebecca Saletan for your early support of this book.

To all of the fantastic women who contributed stories, in particular, Nancy Archuleta, Maria Lourdes de Sobrino, Linda Novey White, and Mercy Makhalemele, thank you.

Your willingness to help others and do so with so much love is inspiring.

To Pat Miller for walking this path with me and coaching me to discover my truth.

To Jim Sinegal for believing in me and for your support in letting me prove I could do it.

To Tony Smith for your unwavering commitment, for taking a stand for me and with me in causing a world we are all proud to leave our children.

To Don Soderquist for listening and sharing your wisdom, for championing me and this project, and for your commitment to ethical leadership.

To the following incredible individuals who came into my life at just the right time. Your encouraging words and actions keep me going:

Stephanie Abruzia	Wayne Easterling
Isabel Allende	Len Edwards
Gina Amaro	Joe Ettore
Bill Blass	Fred Fernandez
Alice Borodkin	Edie Fraser
Facundo Bravo	Frank Gomez
Marion Luna Brem	Earl Graves
Lenny Bruce	Leslie Grossman
Aubyn Burnside	Nanci Hartwick
Christina Caballero	George Herrera
Anna Carbonell	Howard Israel
Vanessa Castagna	Jesse Jackson
Brian Connolly	Jaworski Family
Barbara Corcoran	Andrea Jung
Flora Davidson	Excell Lafayette

Acknowledgments

Gerald Levin

Elizabeth Lisboa-Farrow

Fred Mandell

John Medina

Helen Meyers

Manuel Mirabal

Dr. Mercedes Montealegre

Rose McElrath Slade

Nina McLemore

Jose Niño

Dr. Antonia Novello

Cecilia Pagkalinawan

Bruce Perkins

Coleman Peterson

Ann Portas

Lou Pritchett

Alvin Rohrs

Leila Perez Ross

Cong. Loretta Sanchez

Erin Saxton

Dr. Adele Scheele

Aida de Soto

Phyllis Street

Celia Swanson

Dennis Swanson

Kathy Thebo

Luz Tirado

Geraldo Rivera

Kathleen Walas

Dottie Walters

Rich Warnat

Juanita Weaver

Edie Weiner

Sheila Wellington

Governor Christine Whitman

Ella Williams

Marianne Williamson

Marian Wright Edelman

Raul Yzaguirre

To my teachers along the way for believing in me before I could believe in myself: Mr. Acevedo, Mrs. Riley, Mrs. Lamb-Armstrong, Mujib, Mr. Sherman, Mr. Freeman, Mr. Bischoff. For aiding my journey: Dr. Moon, Dr. Kasper, and Dr. Lanner-Cusin.

To Mary Higbie for her early assistance in this project. And to Fran Gellas and Rita Merring, two of the best people I've ever worked with. Thank you for your willingness to sort it out and get the job done.

To Morris Shaw and Marcia Taylor, thanks for giving me a chance and then helping all along the way.

To Debbie Derella Cheren, your faith and love are a great gift.

To the generations of women on whose shoulders and sacrifices I stand, in particular Emma Rodriguez and Emilia Bernard.

To Grandma Eli for sharing your love and generous soul with me and the boys. You live in our hearts and the wonderful memories we share.

To my sister, Dorcas, who powerfully encouraged me to do it my way.

To my brother, J, for his strength and support.

To my parents for your love, for teaching me the value of hard work and education and for passing on such a rich culture.

To Doreen for your love and understanding. You are the best friend a gal could ever have.

And to Steve for always being there. For your encouragement every step of the way and for your willingness to walk a new path.

And to the three awesome people I have been so lucky to call my sons. I couldn't have done it without your help. Thanks for supporting Mom in her life's work. Every moment has been made more delicious because you're in it. I love you.

And to the tens of thousands of men and women who have shared their stories with me, your willingness to claim your own power and greatness inspires me.

Contact Information for the Women You Read About:

Nancy E. Archuleta, CEO/Chairperson
MEVATEC Corporation
1525 Perimeter Parkway Suite 500
Huntsville, Alabama 35806
256-890-8000 – Phone
256-890-0000 – Fax
nancy.archuleta@mevatec.com

Professional services in engineering, technical, financial management and information technology. Customer base includes U.S. Department of Defense, NASA, state and municipalities, and oil companies. Keynote speaker, leadership and business management. Motivator.

Alice Borodkin, President, Publisher, and Editor-in-Chief
Women's Business Chronicle, Inc.
Women's Network
Zenith Woman Magazine
Denver, CO
303-320-1474 – Phone
303-320-1494 – Fax
aborodkin@womensbizchronicle.com

Marion Luna Brem, President/CEO
Love Chrysler Inc
4331 S. Staples
Corpus Christi, TX 78411
361-991-5683 – Phone
361-991-2351 – Fax
www.LOVECHRYSLER.com

DaimlerChrysler 5 Star award winning auto dealership selling and servicing Chrysler, Dodge and Jeep vehicles. Keynote speaker, motivator and author on topics ranging from breast cancer to being a woman in a male-dominated industry.

Aubyn C. Burnside, CEO/Founder
Suitcases For Kids
P.O. Box 1144
Hickory, NC 28603
828-328-7338 – Fax
www.suitcasesforkids.org

At age 10, Aubyn conceived and founded this international nonprofit that has active chapters in all 50 states and 23 foreign countries. Aubyn is active in 4-H, Girl Scouts, and church youth groups. Now 16, she gives many motivational speeches and is available internationally to address meetings of any size or age.

Barbara Corcoran, Chairman and Founder
The Corcoran Group
660 Madison Avenue
11th Floor
New York, NY 10021
212-355-3550 – Phone
212-303-9711 – Fax
www.corcoran.com

The Corcoran Group Real Estate was founded in 1973. With over 550 brokers, $2 billion in annual sales, and 10 offices, the Corcoran Group is the largest privately owned real estate firm in Manhattan. Corcoran.com was founded in 1995 and has grown to become the world's most comprehensive luxury real estate source with representation in over 100 countries. Barbara Corcoran is viewed as the voice of New York luxury real estate, and her commentary is sought after daily by consumers, brokers, analysts, and the media.

Mercy Makhalemele, Founder
Sisters in Action Center
P.O. Box 18217
Dalbridge 4014
Durban, South Africa

Contact Information

08-3-331-7495 - Phone
mwmakhal@yahoo.com

Sisters in Action, also called Ubumbano LoMama, (women working together) in partnership with AIDSLINK, one of the oldest AIDS service organizations in South Africa, delivers educational workshops and creates community development projects to support women who are HIV+ and women who are affected by HIV.

Sisters in Action was instrumental in organizing a satellite conference on women and HIV at the 13th International AIDS Conference in Durban South Africa.

To help: send funds or request a supplies-needed list.

Rose McElrath-Slade, President & CEO
Strategic Resources, Inc
7700 Leesburg Pike, Suite 108
Falls Church, VA 22043
703-749-3040 – Phone
703-749-3046 – Fax
rslade@sri-hq.com
www.sri-hq.com

Strategic Resources, Inc. (SRI)) is an ISO 9001 certified, international company specializing in management, information technology, telecommunications and logistics/engineering consulting services. Clients include FDA, Departments of Education, Veterans Affairs, Army and Navy, Computer Science Corp (CSC), Freddie Mac, SAIC, MCI and other federal agencies and fortune five hundred companies.

SRI has repeatedly been ranked among fast growing businesses and has been recognized by clients for excellence in services offered.

Pat Miller
Mission Possible, Inc.
1300 Pasadena Ave NE
Atlanta, GA 30306
404-873-2442 – Phone
404-873-2525 – Fax
pat@missionpossibleinc.com
www.missionpossibleinc.com

International coach and consultant in executive and entrepreneurial leadership, organizational and professional development. Mission Possible serves individuals as well as large and small organizations to " make their mission possible. . . to help them remember their greatness. . . to free their genius. . . to turn their potential into performance, creating and realizing the possibilities well within their reach".

Linda Novey White, CEO/Founder
Linda Novey Enterprises, Inc.
5778 Carriage Drive
Sarasota, FL 34243
941-351-1557 – Phone
941-351-1735 – Fax
www.lindanovey.com
www.novey.cc
International consultants in areas of customer service, staff training and motivation, anonymous service audits and strategic planning. Such clients as Ritz-Carlton, Peninsula, Neiman Marcus, Beverly Hills Hotel, and Wall Street Bankers have used the company's services to enhance their core development. Keynote speaker, motivator, humorist.

Cecilia Pagkalinawan, CEO/Founder
BoutiqueY3K, Inc.
275 Seventh Ave, 25th floor
New York, NY 10001
212-727-0520 – Phone
212-727-3697 – Fax
Cecilia@boutiqueY3K.com
www.boutiqueY3K.com

BoutiqueY3K is a leading e-commerce and e-marketing consulting firm specializing in entertainment, media, fashion and luxury goods and services. Clients such as NineWest, BabyGear, Jones Apparel Group, Furla and Showbees have used the company's services to develop their e-businesses.

Rusty Robertson, President & Founder
RPR & Associates
3556 Sweetwater Mesa Road
Malibu, CA 90265
310-317-0355 – Phone
310-456-7554 – Fax
2rpr@bigplanet.com

For over twenty years, RPR & Associates has successfully marketed an eclectic array of companies, celebrities and authors. Listed in Advertising Age's Top 100 Marketers, this marketing and public relations firm specializes in product development, branding and solidifying avenues of distribution.

Congresswoman Loretta Sanchez
U.S. House of Representatives
Washington, DC 20515
202-225-2965 – Phone
202-225-5859 – Fax
Loretta@mail.house.gov
www.house.gov/sanchez
District Office: Garden Grove
District Phone: 714-621-0102

Maria de Lourdes Sobrino, President & CEO
LuLu's Dessert/Fancy Fruit Corporation
5452 Oceanus Drive
Huntington Beach, CA 92649
714-895-5483 - Phone
714-373-2350 - Fax
mariasobrino@lulusdessert.com
www.lulusdessert.com
mariasobrino@fancyfruit.com
www.fancyfruit.com

For over 18 years LuLu's Dessert Factory and Fancy Fruit Corporation have successfully created, manufactured, and sold a full line of desserts, particularly ready-to-eat single portion gelatins and Kosher and Halal 100% natural frozen fruit bars.

Contact Information

Phyllis Street, Artist
Purely Appalachia Craft Empowerment (PACE) Program
409 E. Front Street
P.O. Box 1458
Coeburn, VA 24230
(540) 395-5160 - Phone
(540) 395-7804 - Fax
pace@naxs.net
www.purelyappalachiacrafts.com

PACE is a non-profit marketing organization for artisans in the Southwest Virginia coalfield (and surrounding) area. The program strives to preserve and to perpetuate the Appalachian craft heritage. Artists use traditional methods and materials to produce quality crafts, which include, but are not limited to, pottery, woodwork, fibers, weavings, quilts, basketry, toys, and brooms.

Contact Information for the Organizations You Read About:

Business Women's Network (BWN)
1146 19th Street, NW, 3rd Floor
Washington, DC 20036
Edie Fraser, President
202-466-8209 – Phone
202-833-1808 – Fax
Edie@BWNi.com
www.BWNi.com

The Business Women's Network (BWN) founded in 1993, acts as an umbrella organization to unite, network, and promote more than 6,000 women's business, professional organizations and web sites. BWN produces the *BWN Directory*, the *Calendar of Women's Events*, and *Women and Diversity WOW! Facts* in print copy and on-line. This includes a compilation of resources for college women with information on internships, mentoring and career choices.

Children's Defense Fund
25 E. Street, NW
Washington, DC 20001
202-628-8787 – Phone
202-662-3510 – Fax
cdfinfo@childrensdefense.org
www.childrensdefense.org

"The mission of the Children's Defense Fund is to *"Leave No Child Behind"* and to ensure a healthy start, a head start, a fair start, a safe start and a moral start in life and successful passage to adulthood with the help of caring families and communities". CDF began in 1973 and is a private, nonprofit organization supported by foundations, corporate grants and individual donations.

The Committee of 200
625 North Michigan Avenue, Suite 500
Chicago, Illinois 60611-3108
312-751-3477 - Phone
312-943-9401 - Fax
www.c200.org

A professional organization of preeminent businesswomen. Their mission is to "exemplify and promote entrepreneurship and corporate leadership among women of this generation and the next." The Committee of 200 also has a Foundation with mentoring, scholarship and outreach initiatives targeted at emerging entrepreneurs and business students.

Count Me In for Women's Economic Independence
22 West 26th Street, Suite 9H
New York, New York 10010
212-691-6380 – Phone
www.count-me-in.org

Count Me In is a non-profit lending and learning organization that raises money to make loans between $500-$10,000 to qualified women who have nowhere else to turn for that all important first business loan. The first on-line micro-lenders, they use a more woman appropriate credit scoring system, taking into consideration different life situations. You can make a contribution or apply for a loan on their web site or by calling or writing.

Million Mom March
National Office
San Francisco General Hospital
San Francisco, CA 94110
415-821-8200 – Phone
888-989-MOMS – Toll Free
415-821-5811 – Fax
national@millionmommarch.org

The Million Mom March is a national grassroots, chapter-based organization dedicated to preventing gun death and injury and supporting victims and survivors of gun trauma. They work for the adoption of sensible gun laws.

National Association of Women Business Owners (NAWBO)
1411 K Street NW, Suite 1300
Washington, DC 20005
202-347-8686 – Phone
202-347-4130 – Fax
national@nawbo.org

NAWBO is a national, member supported organization representing the interests of women business owners in all industries across the United States. Membership can expand your business opportunities by giving you access to the right people, support and resources. To find a local chapter or get further information, contact the above.

National Puerto Rican Coalition (NPRC)
1700 K Street, NW, Suite 500
Washington, DC 20006
202-223-3915 – Phone
202-429-2223 – Fax
www.bateylink.org

NPRC's mission is to systematically strengthen and enhance the social, political, and economic well-being of Puerto Ricans throughout the United States and in Puerto Rico with a special focus on the most vulnerable. NPRC works through a national network of hundreds of community based organizations.

NJ Advisory Commission on the Status of Women
Division on Women
New Jersey Department of Community Affairs
101 South Broad Street, Box 801
Trenton, NJ 08625
609-292-8840 – Phone
609-633-6821 – Fax

The mission of the New Jersey Commission on the Status of Women is to advise the Division on Women on the needs and concerns of all the women of New Jersey; and to advocate, promote and support equality for women. Most states have a commission on the status of women and can be a one-stop shopping source of local help and resources. Check online or in your local yellow pages.

Oseola McCarty Scholarship Fund
University of Southern Mississippi
Public Relations
Box 10026
Hattiesburg, Mississippi 39406
601-266-4491 – Phone
601-266-5347 – Fax
www.pr.usm.edu/oolamain.htm

To contribute to or get further information about the Oseola McCarty Scholarship Fund, contact the above address.

Students in Free Enterprise (SIFE)
The Jack Shewmaker SIFE World Headquarters
1959 East Kerr Street
Springfield, MO 65803-4775
800-677-SIFE – Phone
417-831-6165 – Fax
sifehq@sife.org
www.SIFE.org

Founded in 1975, SIFE is one of the world's largest non-profit free enterprise organizations. Active on more than 800 college campuses in twenty countries, SIFE's mission is to provide college students the best opportunity to make a difference and to develop leadership, teamwork and communication skills through learning, practicing and teaching the principles of free enterprise. SIFE teams teach business concepts such as budgeting, accounting, and supply and demand. They help budding entrepreneurs get their plans off the ground and mentor at-risk students, inspiring them to reach for their dreams.

United States Hispanic Chamber of Commerce (USHCC)
2175 K Street NW, Suite 100
Washington, DC 20037
202-842-1212 – Phone
202-842-3221 – Fax
www.ushcc.com

The mission of the USHCC is to advocate, promote and facilitate the success of Hispanic businesses. An umbrella organization for nearly 250 chambers throughout the U.S., the USHCC actively promotes the economic growth and development of Hispanic entrepreneurs. For further information on a variety of programs including procurement opportunities, access to capital, SDB certification and youth entrepreneurship, visit their website.

United States Small Business Administration
409 Third Street, SW
Washington, DC 20416
202-205-6673 – Phone
202-205-7064 – Fax
800-U-ASK-SBA - Toll free SBA answer desk
704-344-6640- TDD
www.sba.gov
www.sba.gov/womeninbusiness

The USSBA provides "financial, technical and management assistance to help American start, run and grow their businesses." Their services are too numerous to list here but include business counseling, government guaranteed loans and capital. In addition, they have over 65 Women's Business Centers throughout the country providing help with all aspects of business ownership.

Wal-Mart Minority/Women-Owned Business
Development Program
Wal-Mart Stores, Inc.
702 Southwest 8th Street
Bentonville, AR 72716
Contact: Excell Lafayette, Jr.
501-277-1766 – Phone
501-277-2532 – Fax
elafaye@wal-mart.com

If you're interested in becoming a Wal-Mart supplier and own a minority and/or woman-owned business, you should apply to Wal-Mart's Minority & Women-Owned Business Development Program. The program requires that you are certified or in the certification process through either the National Minority Supplier Development Council or the Women's Business Enterprise National Council.

Most major corporations have similar initiatives.
To learn more, visit their corporate websites.

The Women's Alliance
2650 SW 27th Avenue, Suite #202
Miami, FL 33133
305-444-7020 – Phone
305-444-3778 – Fax
info@thewomensalliance.org

A bridge to opportunity and independence, the Women's Alliance is a not-for-profit membership alliance of independent community based organizations that increase the employability of low-income women by providing professional attire, career skills training, and a range of support services from dental care to health and wellness programs.

How to help: Reach into your purse, clean out your closet,
volunteer, launch your own program, tell a friend,
organize an accessory drive at your office.

Women Presidents' Organization (WPO)
598 Broadway, 6th Floor
New York, NY 10012
212-941-8510 - Phone
212-941-9575 - Fax
info@womenpresidentsorg.com

The WPO is an exclusive professional development and peer advisory group for successful entrepreneurial women. Each WPO member has already met the challenge of guiding a business to at least $2 million in annual sales (if product driven), or $1 million (if service driven). Meetings are coordinated by a professional facilitator.

Women's Venture Fund, Inc.
240 West 35th Street, Suite 201
New York, NY 10001

Contact Information

212-563-0499 – Phone
212-868-9116 – Fax
info@womensventurefund.org

Women's Venture Fund (WVF) is a not-for-profit organization dedicated to the development of women owned small businesses by combining training, funding, and mentoring. WVF offers micro loans up to $15,000 to low-income women in underserved communities exclusively in New York City. They help women who are unable to obtain loans through traditional financial institutions. WVF has plenty of outside resources they can refer you to if you have a business outside of New York City.

ABOUT CHILD SEXUAL ABUSE:

The American Academy of Pediatrics reports that sexual abuse "is more common than most people realize. At least 1 out of 5 adult women and 1 out of 10 adult men report having been sexually abused in childhood." By better educating yourself and your children, you can help prevent it from happening and better cope with it if it does.

For further information, please contact:

Prevent Child Abuse America
PO Box 2866
Chicago, IL 60604-2404
312-663-3520-Phone
312-939-8962-Fax
800-556-2722- Toll Free Information Line
www. preventchildabuse.org

ABOUT BECOMING AN ORGAN DONOR:

Currently, more than 65,000 Americans are waiting for a life saving organ transplant. Tragically, every day 12 people will die while waiting. And every 16 minutes another name is added to the waiting list. Thankfully, one donor can help more than 50 people in need.
To help, you can contact your local coalition for a donor card or call for a free brochure on donation by dialing
1-800-355-SHARE.

Coalition on Donation
1100 Boulder Parkway, Suite 500
Richmond, VA 23225-8770
804-330-8620 – Phone
804-330-8593 - Fax
www.shareyourlife.org

TO GET MENTAL HEALTH INFORMATION:

For free materials on a variety of mental health topics and referrals to local organizations and support groups contact:

National Mental Health Association (NMHA)
1021 Prince Street
Alexandria, VA 22314-2971
703-684-7722 – Phone
703-684-5968 – Fax
800-969-NHMA – toll free information line
800-433-5959 – TTY line
www.nmha.org

Index

Index

Index

About the Author

DEBORAH ROSADO SHAW is an award-winning entrepreneur, keynote speaker, civic leader, and mother of three.

Her strategies for success have been profiled in *Business Week, Forbes, USA Today,* and on CNN and NBC. Ms. Shaw's achievements have been used as a case study in several textbooks.

Ms. Shaw advises the CEOs and top executives of several Fortune 100 retail, banking, and food companies on issues ranging from marketing to diversity. She is also a twice-appointed commissioner with the New Jersey Commission on the Status of Women.

An international speaker on issues of personal empowerment, business strategy, and entrepreneurship, Ms. Shaw has inspired tens of thousands of people from all walks of life.

She is the founder of Dream BIG! Enterprises, LLC., and the founder and CEO of Umbrellas Plus, LLC, a multi-million dollar wholesaler and importer of fashion and sun accessories. Her clients have included Avon, Costco, Kraft General Foods, Toys "R" Us and Wal-Mart.

Ms. Shaw lives in New Jersey with her family.

DEBORAH WOULD LOVE TO HEAR FROM YOU

To share a success story or your comments, please email:
deb@edreambig.com

Also, if you would like to:

- Submit a story for inclusion in a forthcoming Dream BIG! book
- Enter to win the Dream BIG! contest
- Get information about booking Deborah for your next event
- Learn when the Dream BIG! tour is coming to a city near you
- Get Deborah's recommended reading list
- Be added to the Dream BIG! mailing list

WE INVITE YOU TO VISIT OUR WEBSITE AT:
www.edreambig.com

OR COPY THIS FORM AND MAIL IT TO:

Dream BIG! Enterprises, LLC.
Post Office Box 100
Chester, New Jersey 07930

Name (please print) . . . .

Address . . . .

City . . . . State . . . . . Zip . . . .

Phone number . . . .

Email address . . . .